ARE YOU RAPTURE READY?

ARE YOU
RAPTURE
READY?

Signs, Prophesies, Warnings, Threats, and
Suspicions that the Endtime Is Now

TODD STRANDBERG

AND

TERRY JAMES

DUTTON

DUTTON
Published by Penguin Group (USA) Inc.
375 Hudson Street, New York, New York 10014, U.S.A.
Penguin Books Ltd, Registered Offices: 80 Strand, London WC2R 0RL, England
Penguin Books Australia Ltd, 250 Camberwell Road, Camberwell,
Victoria 3124, Australia
Penguin Books Canada Ltd, 10 Alcorn Avenue, Toronto, Ontario, Canada M4V 3B2
Penguin Books (NZ) Ltd, Cnr Rosedale and Airborne Roads, Albany,
Auckland 1310, New Zealand

Published by Dutton, a member of Penguin Group (USA) Inc.

First printing, June 2003
1   3   5   7   9   10   8   6   4   2

Excerpts from the *Left Behind* series by Tim LaHaye and Jerry B. Jenkins
reprinted by permission of Tyndale House.

 REGISTERED TRADEMARK—MARCA REGISTRADA

LIBRARY OF CONGRESS CATALOGING-IN-PUBLICATION DATA

Strandberg, Todd.
Are you rapture ready? : signs, prophecies, warnings, threats, and
suspicions that the endtime is now / by Todd Strandberg and Terry James.

p.   cm.
ISBN 0-525-94737-X (alk. paper)
1. Rapture (Christian eschatology)   I. James, William T., 1942–   II. Title.
BT887 .S76 2003
236'.9—dc21   2003000138

Printed in the United States of America
Set in Adobe Garamond
Designed by Ellen Cipriano

ACKNOWLEDGMENTS

Our sincere thanks to all those at Dutton who have poured their toil and creativity into this book's production.

Our deep appreciation to Angie Peters for her indispensable day-to-day editorial involvement in the research and writing of the book.

Our profound gratitude to Dr. Tim LaHaye for his great generosity in providing the book's Foreword, and for his longtime friendship.

To the reader of *Are You Rapture Ready?*, our prayers and best wishes.

Most of all, our thanks to our Lord Jesus Christ, to Whom belongs all honor, power, and glory forever.

CONTENTS

FOREWORD

Are you "Rapture ready"? Considering the times in which we live, there can be no question of greater significance. In this book, authors Todd Strandberg and William Terry James have carefully scrutinized the Scriptures as well as sifted through the latest trends and philosophies to bring you a compelling and thorough examination of this fascinating and controversial biblical theme.

It was at my father's funeral many years ago that I first heard about the Rapture. His death had been the result of a sudden heart attack, and I was devastated. The minister quoted 1 Thessalonians 4:13–17, the famous Rapture passage. He concluded with verse 18: *"Therefore comfort one another with these words."* From that day forward, I never lost sight of the Rapture and its powerful ability to bring comfort.

Utilizing excerpts from our *Left Behind* series as a springboard, Strandberg and James tackle the subject of the Rapture with insight and humor. It is a welcome approach that many seekers of truth will find helpful as they try to gain an understanding of this mysterious event that was prophesied thousands of years ago in the Word of

God. With clarity, the authors cut through the confusion and contradictory theories floating around today. Their aim is to bring you to a place of discernment regarding this approaching milestone in human history. It is a glorious event that Christians have hoped for and longed for down through the centuries. Now we stand, having entered the new millennium, with the possibility of this miraculous phenomenon occurring in our lifetime. Yes, it is an exciting time to be alive!

Whatever questions you may have regarding the Rapture, you should find them answered here. It is my fervent prayer that, after reading the pages of this book, you, yourself, will be able to answer that all-important question, *"Are you rapture ready?"* . . . with a definitive *"Yes!"*

Dr. Tim LaHaye

INTRODUCTION

Her knees buckled as she tried to speak, and her voice came in a whiny squeal.

"People are missing," she managed in a whisper, burying her head in his chest.

He took her shoulders and tried to push her back, but she fought to stay close. "What do you mean—?"

She was sobbing now, her body out of control. "A whole bunch of people, just gone!"

"Hattie, this is a big plane. They've wandered to the lavs or—"

She pulled his head down so she could speak directly into his ear. Despite her weeping, she was plainly fighting to make herself understood. "I've been everywhere. I'm telling you, dozens of people are missing."

"Hattie, it's still dark. We'll find—"

"I'm not crazy! See for yourself! All over the plane, people have disappeared."

—Tim LaHaye and Jerry B. Jenkins, *Left Behind*

Fans of the *Left Behind* novels began following every plot twist and turn from the time Tim LaHaye and Jerry Jenkins's first book hit the market. The epic story begins with a singular prophetic event. Millions of readers became familiar with the term for this predicted occurrence. Yet its true nature remains a mystery.

RAPTURE!

Bible prophecy foretells an event that will stagger the world. That event will, the Holy Scriptures say, happen suddenly and without warning. It can happen at any moment.

The *Left Behind* novels made the term almost a household word among vast numbers of people across America. Strangely, however, although it is the real star of the *Left Behind* series, the Rapture remains largely misunderstood—or not understood at all.

Most who are not Christians, but who know a little bit about the subject from the *Left Behind* books, look at the Rapture as a topic of curiosity and entertainment. And for many within the Christian religion, the Rapture either sparks the same kind of fascination or it generates little interest at all.

For most, the subject is a big question mark.

At the same time, the prophesied phenomenon called the Rapture has caused division among many who classify themselves as Christians. Merely mentioning the word "Rapture" brings angry or mocking indignation from some. Others know the Rapture as truth that makes the character of God come alive.

The Rapture Magnet

The word "Rapture" isn't found in the Bible at all. Why, then, has it spawned such great controversy among various segments of Christianity? What is the magnetism that draws believers and nonbelievers alike to fascination with the event? What is it all about? Where did the idea come from? Is it something that is really going to happen? If so, when? How will it affect us?

WHAT IN THE WORLD WILL HAPPEN NEXT?

The Bible has much to say about things yet future. The Rapture is key to those prophesied things remaining to be fulfilled. *Are You Rapture Ready? Signs, Prophecies, Warnings, Threats, and Suspicions that the Endtime Is Now* will lead you through an adventure of discovery about what is predicted for Planet Earth. It will, we sincerely believe, give greater meaning and understanding to the many, often troubling, and sometimes frightening, things you may have read about in the *Left Behind* fictional accounts.

Foreshocks of Apocalypse

The Bible gives no specific prophetic signs that will precede the Rapture. It will be unannounced. Instantaneous. World-stunning. The Bible's prophets, on the other hand, list many prophetic signs that will precede the seven-year period of world trouble known as "Tribulation," or "Apocalypse." Interestingly enough, prophecy scholars are finding that signs similar to those Bible prophets gave for the Tribulation era are all around us today.

These signals, the Bible prophets said, will happen simultaneously and increase in frequency and intensity with each day that passes. The signs will prove that human history, as it has been known, will have entered its final seven years. The Second Coming of Christ will then take place.

Some Peace Treaty . . .

Before the last seven years begin, there must come a treaty of peace between Israel and its enemies. This, Bible prophecy says, will be a seven-year security arrangement for peace, guaranteed by a particular world leader. Israel's agreement to join in this peacemaking will, prophecy predicts, set in motion the time of Tribulation. That era will be marked by an incremental intensifying of God's judgment upon the Earth. We know for sure that this peace hasn't been made. Each newscast that announces a suicide bombing reminds us that it hasn't yet happened.

So while we know that the Apocalypse has not yet begun, we see signs given for that last seven years—including a Middle East peace process—appearing in our headlines daily.

QUESTIONS AND MORE QUESTIONS

What does it all mean? If there are no signs to look for before the Rapture, and the signs for the Tribulation are here now, increasing with frequency and intensity, what are we to make of it?

Exactly what are these signals of the Tribulation and of the Second Coming of Christ? What does Israel becoming a nation again on a single day, May 14, 1948, after almost two thousand years, mean in terms of Bible prophecy?

Why is the rise of the European Union so important?

How was the Soviet Union's falling apart significant?

Does prophecy have anything to say about China?

Is America a part of end-time scenarios?

How much like the prophesied end-time economic situations is today's volatile economy?

Was the religious fanaticism and murderous terrorism we see in the news daily forecasted for the last days?

Do the fantastic increases in technology involving computers and speed of travel have anything to do with prophecy?

UFOs: Are they real? What do their appearings and disappearings mean?

Who is the world leader who can make peace between Israel and its enemies—something no other politician or statesman has come close to doing?

What part does the Rapture play in the end-time scheme of things?

More to the point: How will all of these things personally affect you? Why is the Rapture important to you, your family and friends?

Some Intriguing Answers

This book looks closely at the amazing event called the Rapture. It proposes answers to what is going on all around us today, and what these profound matters have to do with Bible prophecy. *Are You Rapture Ready?* is not only the title of a book relevant to our time; it is a question that each individual should be asking himself or herself.

Rapture is not a harbinger of frightening things to come. It is a giant leap of glorious dimensions. It will take place just before mankind reaches the entrance to the dark, end-time tunnel of Tribulation. Bible prophecy calls the Rapture "the blessed hope" (Titus 2:13).

ARE YOU RAPTURE READY?

CHAPTER 1

End-Time Signs?
Or Just Plain Silliness?

The little old bald cartoon guy with the long white beard, wearing a flowing robe cinched at the waist by a piece of rope, comes to mind. He carries a sign on a large square of white cardboard tacked to a length of wood. The caricature prophet's placard reads THE END IS NEAR!

Prophecy, particularly Bible prophecy, has long been viewed in this fun-poking way by the humorists of modern times. Talk of Apocalypse, Armageddon, and the Second Coming has always been met with raised eyebrows and wry smiles of amused tolerance for the "utter nonsense."

Those who believe in prophecy as reality predicted well in advance, however, come in many varieties. There are the religionist prophecy buffs. There are the nonreligious spiritualists. There are cultists and occultists who claim knowledge of things to come. And there are students of the Bible who look for truth in the Word of God.

THE TIMES, THEY ARE A-CHANGIN'

The "cool" view of what is considered sham fortune-telling at best, and mad ravings at worst, pigeonholes all who delve into prophecy in the same "kook" classification . . . Under *normal* circumstances, that is . . .

"The times," however—as somebody *really* cool once said—"they are a-changin'." World circumstances now come in strange shades of issues and events that jolt our daily lives like never before. Abnormal circumstances have, since September 11, 2001, seemingly become the norm. Americans, for example, now live under various color codes of national security alert status.

The Pew-Power of Prophecy

Everybody—well, almost everybody—attended Mass, church, or synagogue following the horrendous terrorist devastation in New York and Washington, D.C.

"After the attack, millions of nominally churched or generally irreligious Americans were desperately seeking something that would restore stability and a sense of meaning to life," commented George Barna, who directed a study called "How America's Faith Has Changed Since 9-11" (November 26, 2001, www.barna.org).

Suddenly, the word "God" was appearing everywhere. "God bless America" became a rallying cry that ranked up there with the American flag and the Pledge of Allegiance. Ray Charles's version of "America" took on as much patriotic gravitas as "The Star Spangled Banner." When an atheist who had a daughter in elementary school sued to have the words "under God" removed from the Pledge of Allegiance, the usually lethargic—some even say, slothful—Congress immediately began moving to assure the removal could never happen.

For a time at least, people sought answers to the nagging questions they couldn't even really define. They only knew that the terrorist threats originated in the Middle East, and that the events had something to do with the centuries-old problems between Israel and its enemies.

Armageddon Anxiety

Armageddon? Doesn't the Bible say something about a battle called Armageddon? Isn't that conflict supposed to take place somewhere near Israel? And isn't that to lead to the end of the world?

Every time things heat up in the Holy Land, even the mainstream news organizations of the world start talking about Armageddon. From Egyptian President Gamal Abdel Nasser's 1956 war to destroy Israel, to the 1990–1991 Iraqi Scud missile attacks on Israel by Saddam Hussein, every hostility involving Israel has brought fears of igniting the biblically prophesied conflagration.

End-Time Terrorism?

Terrorist acts against Israel have never ceased. These attacks have increasingly involved assaults on U.S. interests. Embassies were invaded, with hostages held for 444 days; ships were attacked while in harbor; military barracks were blown apart—America has increasingly felt the terroristic wrath.

Still, Israel bore the brunt of the terrorists' hatred. Civilians were more often the terrorists' favorite targets than the Israeli military.

Yasser Arafat's terrorist organization, Black September, for example, murdered eleven Israeli athletes during the 1972 Munich Olympic Games.

Then the attacks began to really hit home. The World Trade Center was first bombed in 1993. The twin World Trade towers, symbolizing America's and the world's economic strength and stability, were next struck in 2001. This time they collapsed into flaming rubble. The Pentagon, symbol of U.S. military power, was also dealt a deadly blow. The fanatics who did it originated from the place where Armageddon was prophesied to be fought.

Suddenly the idea of prophecy—especially Bible prophecy—didn't seem quite so ridiculous as before the attacks, when America had stood proud, unscathed, and unafraid.

Back to Business—Well, Kind Of

Things settled down again, like they always do. Church and synagogue attendance soon returned to normal after September 11, 2001. In fact, church attendance was reported to be at pre-attack levels by November of the same year.

"[People] tended to appreciate the moments of comfort they received, but were unaware of anything sufficiently unique or beneficial as to redesign their lifestyle to integrate a deeper level of spiritual involvement," notes Barna ("How America's Faith Has Changed Since 9-11," November 26, 2001, www.barna.org).

Despite economic reverberations caused by the strike against one of the world's financial headquarters, Wall Street and the other economic nerve centers of Planet Earth got back to their wild ride up and down the stock market roller coaster.

Yet there remains the distinct sense that something weird is going on. It's as if America and the world are collectively holding their breath, waiting for the other shoe of catastrophe to drop. A sort of geopolitical nervous disorder seems to have infected our world. Could there be something to all of this end-time stuff after all? Or is the talk of prophecy and the last days all just plain silliness?

PAST PROPHETIC PRONOUNCEMENTS

Argument and debate over the authenticity or the foolishness of prophecy have always been with us. Whether arguing the non-biblical prophecies of Nostradamus, Edgar Cayce, and Jeane Dixon or debating the foretellings of the Bible prophets Isaiah, Jeremiah, and Ezekiel, proponents and opponents of prophecy have long fought it out in the arenas of philosophy and theology.

(Our book's title pretty well says it all so far as in which corner we stand. We are dedicated to exploring things involving Bible prophecy. We will stick to looking closely at biblical prophecy in general, and at the Rapture in particular.)

Then and Today: A Comparison

"People have been saying we're living in the last days for years." So goes one of the most repeated arguments against the validity of Bible prophecy. How do we know whether we really are living in the last days? One way to try to find out is to compare prophetic commentary made in the past with events occurring today.

Then: The study of Scripture numerology or "Bible math" was big in the late 1880s. One key mathematical theory stated the time of man would last six thousand years. The starting point was around 4004 B.C. The end of time would have been around A.D. 2000.

Today: It is interesting to note that men who lived more than one hundred years ago forecasted Christ's return in our lifetime, not theirs. They obviously did not see the many prophetic signals we are seeing today. It is ironic that now that the signs are everywhere, most prophecy ministries shy away from prophetic timelines.

Then: In the 1800s, one author commented about the prophesied rebirth of Israel by saying that nearly twenty thousand Jews lived in the Holy Land. It seemed impossible at that time that there would ever again be a Jewish state called Israel.

Today: Israel has been a reality since May 14, 1948, with more than 5 million Jews living there at present.

Then: In past times, prophecy scholars noted that most of the destruction on Earth prophesied to happen during the Tribulation would be coming from God.

Today: With the proliferation of nuclear forces, man himself now has the power to destroy life on Earth.

Then: The idea of a revived Roman Empire, which many today believe to be the developing European Union, had prophecy scholars of the past writing about the city of Rome itself. One talked of all the new construction in the city of Rome as a sign of the revival of the Roman Empire.

Today: The fact that Europe is reforming into the final world government that Daniel and John wrote about in the Bible is unmistakable. The European Union is the driving force behind this reconstitution.

Then: In 1897, the first Zionist movement was held in Switzerland. The birth of this movement caused a stir among prophecy writers of the time. They saw the Jews beginning to think about the return to the Promised Land.

Today: Millions of Jews have returned to Israel from countries in which they have lived for centuries. Most of this relocation has occurred in just the past few years.

Then: In the mid-1930s, one author pointed out that girls in pajama suits dancing barefoot before a Sunday evening congregation was a blatant act that indicated declining morality. The author noted that no one in attendance was unfavorably impressed.

Today: If those dancing girls set themselves ablaze, the fire marshall might be the only one who would care.

Then: Early in the twentieth century, moral decay was evident at the beach, leading one author to observe the costumes that bathers wore and speculate whether nude beaches were on the way.

Today: Nude beaches did come and the bathing suits some wear make you wonder if all beaches could be certified as nude.

Then: Early in the 1900s, modernism was considered "the apostasy"—falling away from Bible truth—of which the

Bible speaks. This modernism lacked leadership and had a general focus to it.

Today: Modernism has become the norm and has branched out manyfold. Higher forms of apostasy are now making inroads. The men of the last century couldn't have foreseen that pagan gods would eventually share equal billing with Jesus, all religions would be moving toward unity, and even God himself would be pronounced dead.

Then: Prophecy scholars of the 1940s saw "modern music" as a sure sign of lawlessness. "Swing music" was cited as appealing to the worst in human nature and for causing people to lose all semblance of self-control.

Today: The music of our time has changed a great deal from the turn of the century. We went from "Elvis the Pelvis" to Madonna and Michael Jackson grabbing themselves on-stage. Many popular singers use four-letter words repeatedly and some, through lyrics, encourage teenagers to commit suicide. The "Age of Rock and Roll" has run the gamut, and left no stone unturned in the pursuit of filth.

RAPTURE'S TIMING UNKNOWN

When Jesus was on Earth around two thousand years ago, He provided man with several warning signs that would herald His return. The Lord intentionally declined to say what exactly would trigger the Rapture of the Church and the start of the Tribulation.

According to the Word of God, the timing of the Rapture is just as much an unknown in Heaven as it is on Earth. Jesus stated clearly, as recorded in Matthew 24:36, "But of that day and hour no one knows, not even the angels of heaven, but My Father only."

It is highly doubtful that there is a tote board in Heaven counting down the days to the Rapture. If the devil were to know the timing of that event, he would certainly initiate a frenzy of demonic activity just ahead of it.

Remember that no prophecy in the Bible gives us an exact date, but many passages offer a general warning of the Endtime.

DECLINING MORALITY DECLARED DEADLY

The Apostle Paul says in 2 Timothy 3:13 that in the last days, "evil men and imposters will grow worse and worse." This decline in morality has always been a favorite topic of prophecy writers. They cite example after example of decadence as solid proof we are getting close to the Tribulation hour.

As our society grows increasingly wicked, it becomes more likely that God will reach a point where He decides to punish Earth's evil. The Almighty's reaction to the decadent cities of Sodom and Gomorrah provide us with strong evidence that He is very sensitive to the levels of immorality.

Can we measure our moral decline in an effort to see where we stand in relationship to the Endtime? Using examples of depravity as a guide to where we are on the prophetic timeline is not as easy as most people might think. Everyone knows there has always been iniquity in the world. The debate is mostly over which way sin is trending.

Desensitized Morality Meter

The biggest obstacle to measuring changes in morality is the process of people becoming desensitized to sin. Abundant data proves that divorce, homosexuality, and corporate greed have all increased over the years. Because we quickly become adjusted to social changes like these, the magnitude of moral decline has largely escaped our attention.

How Low Can We Go?

There is a very straightforward way to evaluate immorality as it relates to the end times. It's not a matter of figuring out whether the ship is sinking; the boat is already lying on its side at the bottom of the ocean. Rather, it's a matter of asking: Can we go any lower from here?

- ⊕ **Pornographic Playhouses** It seems the moral content of today's controversial plays couldn't sink much lower. When New York theaters have already featured productions like *Puppetry of the Penis, The Vagina Monologues,* and *Corpus Christi*—a play featuring a homosexual Christ-like figure—it seems impossible that our society could degenerate much further. It's hard to improve on total depravity (reference for *Corpus Christi* play: http://www.atheists.org/flash.line/ play.htm).
- ⊕ **Cyberspace Sinfulness** Pornographic sites saturate the Internet. Web pages that contain sexual imagery draw huge numbers of people.
- ⊕ **Rock Bottom Rock** In the early 1980s, a number of Christian commentators traveled from church to church speak-

ing out against the evils of rock music. Most of their complaints were about the outrageous lifestyles of the musicians. Back then, the worst example of immorality in music could be quoted from the pulpit. Today it would be unthinkable to directly quote these lyrics in a church setting.

⊕ **Rock Bottom Reverend** The three examples just cited could stand as proof enough that we've hit rock bottom, but there's more. Despite the abundance of sin, few people are lamenting the problem. The lack of anger or even annoyance is a strong indication that we've actually hit rock bottom. When it was revealed that the Rev. Jesse Jackson had committed one of the greatest acts of hypocrisy for someone claiming to be a minister, apathy was the public's only reaction. In 1998, at the height of the Monica Lewinsky sex scandal, Jackson journeyed to the White House to provide spiritual counsel to President Clinton. Two years later, it was revealed that during that meeting Jackson had been brazen enough to bring along an assistant who was pregnant with his love child. The *National Enquirer* made known the news of Jackson's affair on a Monday. By Friday of that same week, the liberal media declared the matter closed   (http://dir.salon.com/politics/feature/2001/01/19/jackson/index.html).

⊕ **Rock Bottom Doc** The signs of total collapse in morality are not exclusive to the U.S. In England, Dr. Harold Shipman was found to have killed more than two hundred people placed in his care by injecting them with lethal doses of heroin. Most crimes of this nature involve financial gain or sexual depravity. Shipman's motives seem to be largely a mystery. His ability to kill and then calmly face the relatives

has baffled investigators (http://www.the-shipman-inquiry.
org.uk/ome.asp).

God's Wake-Up Call?

When God judged nations in the Bible, His wrath always fell because people refused to repent of their rebellion. After September
11, 2001, there was a brief argument over whether the terrorist attack had been a judgment from God. If the attack was the Lord trying to get our attention, the message was clearly ignored, as
demonstrated by America's quick return to business as usual. We
can't help but wonder if He will try again soon.

FAST FORWARD TO PROPHECY FUTURE

The Rapture is the prophetic event most relevant to this generation,
so far as this book is concerned. However, it is equally important
that we look closely at other key prophecies scheduled to be fulfilled
from here to eternity. Examining those predictions given by Jesus
and the prophets will give us a good understanding of the end-time
signs.

We will explore every face of the Rapture throughout the rest of
the book. But for now, we'll put that subject on hold while we look
at what will take place after that event. By so doing, we will get a
clear picture of why the Rapture is so important.

WE ARE THE WORLD

"We are the World." That song, performed and taped by a group of recording artists years ago, brings prophecy for the Endtime into full view. Terms like "the family of man," "the global village," and "the big blue marble" have long been a part of global-speak. "If we all can just come together as one big family of man, peace and prosperity will rule" is the philosophy behind globalism. The philosophy is flawed because man, the Bible says, is flawed because of sin. There are always those among us who desire to dominate and take from us whatever they want. The prophesied movement into one-world government— and one-world everything else—is well underway.

Prophesied World Government

The Israelite prophet Daniel prophesied about end-time global government while he was in Babylonian captivity under the great king, Nebuchadnezzar. The prophecy is recorded in Daniel, chapter 2.

NEBUCHADNEZZAR'S DREAM

King Nebuchadnezzar was by far the most powerful king of all time. He had no opposition to whatever he chose to do. He was also just a bit of a spoiled brat. He had a troubled dream one night. It was so realistic that he knew it must have had supernatural significance. Trouble was, he couldn't remember what he had dreamed.

King Gets Mad

Nebuchadnezzar called for his fortune-tellers. Daniel was classified as part of this group, although he was a true prophet of God while the others were mostly con artists. The king commanded his wise men to tell him the dream he had dreamed. They informed him that wasn't a fair request, but if he would tell them the dream, they would help him make sense of it. Nebuchadnezzar became enraged. He called them all charlatans, and told his soldiers to kill them. If they couldn't even tell him the dream he had forgotten, they certainly couldn't interpret the dream itself.

Daniel Delivers on Dream

Daniel requested that one of the guards get him an audience with the king. The young prophet then told Nebuchadnezzar what the king had dreamed, and he gave graphic details of what it meant.

The king, in his dream, had seen a gigantic metallic image of a man more than ninety feet tall and several yards wide. A variety of metals covered the statue. The head was of gold, the chest and arms of silver, the belly and thighs of bronze, and the legs of iron. The monstrosity's feet and toes were made of iron, mixed with clay.

World Government Foretold

Daniel told the king that the image represented the five great kingdoms that would rule upon Earth from that time in history to the end of human government. Nebuchadnezzar was the head of gold, Daniel told the king. He was indeed the king above all kings. That is, he was without peer among all the kings that were to come. The prophet then told the king what the other metals, of descending quality and value, meant. From the pure gold head, to the ten toes of iron mixed with clay, Daniel described the great kingdoms that God said would reign and rule upon Planet Earth.

God's Prophet Accurate!

Daniel's prophecies all proved to be 100 percent accurate as history unfolded. In fact, God's prophets have always been right on target. (Under ancient Jewish law, a prophet less than perfect in prophesying was subject to being stoned.)

Since space is limited here, we will cut to the bottom line.

The ten toes that grew out of the feet of iron would be, Daniel prophesied, the last government on Earth. Since iron represented the Roman Empire, these toes of iron mixed with clay come out of a revived (or reformed) Roman Empire.

We—as well as most all other Bible students who interpret prophecy literally rather than symbolically—believe that the European Union today is that reviving Roman Empire. When fully developed, ten nations of the area that used to make up the heart of the Roman Empire on the continent of Europe will form the nucleus of the last world empire. That government will start out as promising Utopia, but it will end up being the most horrendous dictatorship ever seen on Earth.

The ten toes could also represent ten world economic power spheres ruled over by a singular one-world governing source, whose prophesied infamous leader we'll discuss next.

PROPHESIED WORLD LEADER

Bible prophecy foretells that a dictator far more fierce and murderous than Adolf Hitler, Joseph Stalin, and Mao Tse-tung combined is coming to Planet Earth.

Prophecies about this future führer are found in a number of

FIND IT FAST

places in the Bible, including Daniel, chapters 8, 9, and 11; Matthew, chapter 24; 2 Thessalonians, chapter 2; and Revelation, chapters 13, 17, and 19.

This leader is called by many names in the Bible: "man of sin," "king of fierce countenance," "the prince that shall come," "son of perdition," and "the beast." His most recognizable name is "Antichrist." He has his own number, with which you might be familiar. It is "666." *Left Behind* readers know him as Nicolae Carpathia from Romania.

Daniel 9:26–27 tells that he will be from the region at the center of what was the ancient Roman Empire.

Today, there are always men clawing their way to the top in European politics. Now that the European Union is in place, and developing quickly, Antichrist could step onto the world stage to perform his hypnotic gig.

PROPHESIED WORLD RELIGION

FIND IT FAST

Revelation 17 is all about a one-world religion that will come on the scene in conjunction with the one-world government during the Tribulation. It will combine all religions into one and be led by a "false prophet" (*Find It Fast:* Revelation 13 and 19). The religious beast will force all who are alive on Earth when he comes into power to take a mark, signifying worship of the Antichrist. Refusing to take that mark in the forehead or in the right hand will mean death by beheading.

Today, ecumenical religious summits occur continually in an effort to bring all religions into a one-world configuration. The "Millennium Summit" in New York City held September 6–8, 2000, is one example; it included more than one thousand religious leaders—

UNHOLY TRINITY

Satan, in order to deceive, counterfeits everything God does. The best example is that Satan will present himself as God, the Antichrist as His Son, and the false prophet as the Holy Spirit. This great deception mocks the Trinity. In the Bible, God is the Father, Jesus the Son, and God's spirit is the Holy Spirit.

rabbis, monks, ministers, and swamis—assembled by an interfaith coalition to discuss world peace and religious unity.

PROPHESIED FALSE PEACE

Daniel the prophet foretold that Antichrist would come on the scene offering peace. But he said it will be a "peace that destroys many" people. In Revelation 6 we read that Antichrist will come on the scene promising peace, but that "peace" will ignite the world war called Armageddon. Jesus Christ will come back at the end of that great war with the armies of Heaven to destroy His enemies and establish perfect peace on Earth for the first time since the Garden of Eden.

Today, we read hour by hour the changes in the ongoing peace process in the Middle East. This process involves the very nation and region the Bible prophesies will be engaged in a peace process at the end of human history. This is setting the stage for the false peace to come. Daniel 9:26–27 foretells that false peace, and what it will mean for a totally duped world.

FIND
IT
FAST

PROPHESIED GLOBAL ECONOMIC SYSTEM

FIND
IT
FAST

Chapters 13 and 18 of Revelation tell much about the sort of economy that will mark the end of the age and the Tribulation. All buying and selling will be done by using marks and numbers. Apparently, currency of the conventional type will no longer be a part of world financial transactions.

The use of electronic funds transfer will apparently be the order of that day. Such control will force all people to comply with whatever the masters dictate. If they do not comply, they will not be able to conduct business or buy food, medicine, and other commodities.

Chapter 18 of Revelation, in particular, describes the total control by world government during the Tribulation. Antichrist's great power and authority will come, in large part, from his absolute control over all economic matters. The Bible calls this world economic system "Babylon," tying the end of human history back to Nebuchadnezzar's ancient Babylon.

There can be little argument that such a system of economic control is currently feasible through electronic fund transfer technologies. Computer, satellite, and other communication technologies make the prophecy about one-world economy a thing that could lurk just around the next corner of economic crisis.

PROPHESIED END-TIME TECHNOLOGY

Earth went from a horse-and-buggy world to a space-travel world in less than a century. Technological development at every level continues at unbelievable speeds. Daniel, chapter 12, predicted our very time. God's angel gave the prophet—now an old man—a glimpse of the phenomenal age in which we live today. The sum of man's knowledge was, several years ago, said to be doubling every few years. Now it is said to be doubling every few months. That is, technology makes possible artificial intelligence that is swiftly re-creating itself. It is thereby acquiring new knowledge that is growing exponentially. Technology is prophecy fulfilling before our eyes and ears!

FIND
IT
FAST

PROPHESIED END-TIME SOCIETY

The Apostle Paul prophesied in 2 Timothy, chapter 3, that the end-time generation would be full of evil and wicked behavior.

2 TIMOTHY 3:1–5

The end-time generation, the Apostle Paul said, will live during a time of great danger. People, he said, will be extremely arrogant, braggarts, and blasphemers of God's name. People will have unnatural affection, disobey authority, abuse addictive substances, consider themselves better than others, be intellectually haughty, be fierce, and despise those who do God's true work. Paul said that the end-time generation will claim a form of religion, but will be totally against God and His chosen way of conduct for mankind.

Our newscasts punctuate the truth of Paul's snapshot of end-time man. Every symptom inundates our society today.

JESUS LAYS OUT LAST-DAYS SIGNS

Disciples of Jesus, while He walked the Earth, were a lot like people of our generation. They lived more for the moment than for the next life.

When, a few days before His crucifixion, they brought Jesus to Mount Olivet overlooking the beautiful temple Herod the Great had refurbished, they were quite proud of it and sought words of its praise from Jesus.

Rather than lavishing praise, as they expected, Jesus told them that a time was coming when not one stone of the temple they were looking at would be left standing atop another. Amazed and worried by this statement, they asked when these things would be and what signs would precede the end of the world.

FIND IT FAST

Jesus answered by laying out specific signals that would lead to His Second Coming to Earth. (*Find It Fast:* Jesus' prophetic message is recorded in the Olivet discourse accounts found in Matthew, chapter 24; Mark, chapter 13; and Luke, chapter 21.)

Christ gave these end-time signals:

⊕ wars and rumors of wars
⊕ false prophets and false teachers
⊕ ethnic hatred
⊕ starvation, disease, and earthquakes
⊕ Israel being at the center of the world's attention

Jesus foretold that there would be wars and rumors of wars throughout history. As in all of His Olivet prophecies, He implied that what He prophesied would increase in frequency and intensity, the nearer the time of His Second Coming.

Wars and Rumors of Wars

Wars and rumors of wars have always reared their ugly heads. Never have there been more than a couple of hundred years without war. The twentieth century was the bloodiest of all, according to historians. Hitler murdered 6 million Jews, plus killed all others he hated; Stalin killed 30 million of his own people in his purges; and Mao slaughtered more than 60 million of his people. The historians obviously are right on this one.

With the terroristic mind-set in full bloom, and the horrific weaponry available to the world's armies, can there be any doubt that Christ's prophecy about wars will be fulfilled? Armageddon, as anyone who observes Mideast madness can see, sits ominously on the horizon.

Jesus said false prophets and false teachers would come, claiming to represent Christ, or claiming to actually be Christ.

False Prophets, False Teachers

It took less than a decade following His crucifixion for Jesus' words to start coming true in this matter. Many sects claiming to be allied to the Christian faith arose during the years immediately following Christ's death, burial, and resurrection. Leaders of these cults claimed everything from being prophets to being the actual Messiah, come to rescue everybody from Roman control.

Rome, of course, didn't like this, and everyone suffered greatly. Most Jews fled for their lives, just as Jesus had predicted. Thousands died upon crosses, in mocking acknowledgment of those being crucified, whom the Roman authorities saw as the disruptive, threatening Christian element. Of course, true Christians had nothing to do with the insurgency.

Jesus, in His prophecy, however, was also speaking to the generation of the time just before His Second Coming. Today, television programming with Christian content is vastly made up of preachers and teachers who gear their messages toward gathering as much money as possible. They make claims of God-promised prosperity. They proclaim that God promises many things that He does not, according to what the Bible has to say. They come in the name of Christ, but their messages most often reflect their love of money. Jesus' prophecy of false prophets and false teachers is evident today.

MATTHEW 24:7; MARK 13:8; LUKE 21:10

One of the most remarkable prophecies of Christ's Olivet discourse is the prophecy that "nation will rise against nation."

The Greek word for "nation" here is *ethnos*. This is "ethnic" in English. Jesus foretold that at the end of human history there would be a tremendous increase in hatred involving ethnic or racial differences.

Ethnic Hatred

While race has often been the basis for wars, modern times have seen the worst cases of ethnic genocide in the history of man. "Ethnic cleansing" has become a common phrase in today's news jargon.

Whether considering Hitler's "Final Solution" involving the genocide against the Jewish race, or the racial atrocities of the Balkan conflict, or the ongoing Arab-Jewish undeclared war, Jesus' words about nations in conflict remain at the forefront of today's news.

Starvation, Disease, Earthquakes

Greater reporting of these disasters, since the advent of instant, worldwide satellite television coverage, puts the dire circumstances of the people affected by them in front of our eyes hourly. Ethiopia, Somalia, the Sudan, and dozens of other regions display apocalyptic conditions to a world that grows desensitized to the tragedies. Earthquakes are reported, due to advances in seismic technologies, as at no time in history. Many seismologists believe the earthquakes are coming in greater numbers, magnitude, and in more diverse locations than ever before.

These things are scheduled, according to Jesus, to become humanly unbearable during the Tribulation. The disasters we are seeing today signal how near we might be to Earth's final days.

MATTHEW 24:7; MARK 13:8; LUKE 21:11

These three things are a natural part of the human condition. Bible prophecy foretells a time that these triplets of calamity will become supernatural rather than natural in origin. These will come in wave after wave upon rebellious mankind during the Tribulation.

Israel Focus of World Attention

The world has been watching Israel with interest and worry since its rebirth as a nation on May 14, 1948. We watch daily while Israel sprouts its leaves of end-time interaction with its hostile neighbors and the rest of the nations of the world.

MATTHEW 24:32; LUKE 21:20

Jesus spoke directly of prophetic things as they relate to the nation of Israel. His Olivet discourse put Israel (the Jewish race) at the heart of His presentation of end-time signs. He also used the prophecies to involve the rest of the people of the world. Additionally, Christ used double reference with regard to time frames. He spoke of times immediately surrounding His death, burial, and resurrection, and of a future time far distant.

He said to watch the fig tree carefully. This is a symbolic reference to Israel. When it begins to put forth its leaves, He said, then people are to know that His coming is very near. Israel will, Jesus prophesied, be at the center of world attention just before He returns to put an end to man's rule over Earth.

THE PROPHET? OR THE OSTRICH?

Some, no doubt, see us as the little bald cartoon prophet with the white, flowing beard and the placard reading THE END IS NEAR! That's okay. We sometimes look back and see skeptics as the proverbial ostrich with its head in the sand.

The issues and events of our times look eerily like end-time world conditions foretold by Jesus and the Bible prophets. We sincerely believe the Rapture can take place at any moment.

Of course, just because we believe it, doesn't make it so. However, just because the skeptics say a Rapture is silly, and won't happen, doesn't mean it won't.

We'll stick with what the Bible, which we know to be the very Word of God, says about the matter. We truly want you to be "Rapture ready."

END-TIME AILMENTS AND RAPTURE-READY RX

Prophecy Denialitis Refusal to believe that we are drawing closer to the Endtime. Inability or unwillingness to give the Bible credit for predicting the rebirth of Israel and the revival of the Roman Empire.

Symptoms Sufferers of this are often nonbelievers. They have little or no knowledge of the books of Daniel or Revelation, and they express no reaction to end-time warning signs.

Treatment Should spend an hour each day reading the Bible and articles on being "Rapture ready." "Be diligent to present yourself approved to God, a worker who does not need to be ashamed, rightly dividing the word of truth" (2 Timothy 2:15).

GET RIGHT,
OR
GET LEFT!

CHAPTER 2

Going Up!
Don't Miss This Elevator!

Local television stations from around the world reported bizarre occurrences, especially in time zones where the event had happened during the day or early evening. CNN showed via satellite the video of a groom disappearing while slipping the ring onto his bride's finger. A funeral home in Australia reported that nearly every mourner disappeared from one memorial service, including the corpse, while at another service at the same time, only a few disappeared and the corpse remained. Morgues also reported corpse disappearances. At a burial, three of six pallbearers stumbled and dropped a casket when the other three disappeared. When they picked up the casket, it, too, was empty.

—Left Behind

STRANGER THAN FICTION

The *Left Behind* novel depicts the Rapture in colorful, sensational, and totally accurate fashion. Millions of people will disappear in a fraction of a second. Even the dead will vanish. Nothing will be left of them except the clothing, shoes, and jewelry they wore, and prosthetics they used.

Sounds crazy, but that's precisely what Bible prophecy indicates will happen:

⊕ Paul the apostle prophesied: "Behold, I tell you a mystery: We shall not all sleep, but we shall all be changed—in a moment, in the twinkling of an eye, at the last trumpet. For the trumpet will sound, and the dead will be raised incorruptible, and we shall be changed" (1 Corinthians 15:51–52).

⊕ Expanding on this prophecy, Paul said in 1 Thessalonians 4:15–17: "For this we say to you by the word of the Lord, that we who are alive and remain until the coming of the Lord will by no means precede those who are asleep. For the Lord Himself will descend from heaven with a shout, with the voice of an archangel, and with the trumpet of God. And the dead in Christ will rise first. Then we who are alive and remain shall be caught up together with them in the clouds to meet the Lord in the air. And thus we shall always be with the Lord."

RAPTURE REVEALED

A major argument against the "Rapture theory," as termed by those who say it will not happen, is that the word "rapture" appears nowhere in the Bible. The statement is partly true; the word appears nowhere in the English Bible. The argument that there is to be no Rapture because the event isn't mentioned by name in the Bible, however, is not valid. This logic fails because a huge number of words don't appear in the Bible, including the word "Bible." Because God's Word was originally written in Hebrew and Greek, one could truthfully say that no English words are in the Bible.

It's All Greek to Us!

Take a look at 1 Thessalonians 4:16–18 in the original Greek.

οτι αυτοσ ο κυριοσ εν κελευσματι εν φωνη αρχαγγελου και εν σαλπιγγι θεου καταβησεται απ ουρανου και οι νεκροι εν χριστω αναστησονται πρωτον 4:17 επειτα ημεισ οι ζωντεσ οι περιλειπομενοι αμα συν αυτοισ αρπαγησομεθα εν νε αισ εισ απαντησιν του κυριου εισ αερα και ουτωσ παντοτε συν κυριω εσομεθα 4:18 ωστε παρακαλειτε αλληλουσ εν τοισ λογοισ τουτοισ29

We don't see the dead in Christ rising, Jesus descending from Heaven, and us meeting Him in the air. So the cynics are right: the word "rapture" is nowhere to be found. All we see is gobbledygook.

Then why the word "rapture"? The word is taken from the

Latin verb *rapere*, which is translated in the English Bible in 1 Thessalonians 4:17 as "caught up." *Harpazo* is the Greek word that the New Testament translators have rendered as "caught up." For example, in 2 Corinthians 12:2, we read of someone being "caught up"—translated from the Greek *harpazo*—to the third heaven. "Rapture" is taken from an obsolete French word that means "abduction" or "to carry off." Though Greek scholars may not use "rapture" to translate *harpazo,* it is not difficult, nor is it doing a disservice to God's Word, to connect the two terms.

In other words, Christian prophecy scholars simply chose to use the English translation of the Latin word from the Latin Bible to come up with the word for the "catching up" of Christians. They chose the Latin verb form over the Greek verb for naming it.

The Apostle Paul's words make it clear that something sudden and spectacular is scheduled to happen. With 1 Thessalonians 4:16–18 giving us such a vivid description of the Rapture, you would have to conclude that some people are just playing games with the Word of God. We could change the name of the "Rapture

Ready" Web site to "Catching Up Ready," but that would hardly improve things.

Reason for Rapture

We can't understand the reason there will be a Rapture unless we first realize why there will be a Tribulation at the end of the present Earth Age. That seven-year period will be a time of judgment on people who have refused to accept the gift of Christ's death, burial, and resurrection as payment for their sin.

Why does turning down that gift bring on such bad news? Here's why: Human beings were created without sin. Perfect. But Adam and Eve, the father and mother of us all, disobeyed their Creator, God, bringing sin into the world. That sin separated men from God and explains the terrorism, murders, and other evils of every kind that have taken place ever since.

But sin can't enter Heaven because it's a place of perfection. When we die, therefore, we sin-tainted creatures certainly can't get in unless we are first cleansed of that sin. That cleansing is made possible through Jesus' death on the cross at Calvary. At His death, all of our sin was judged by God and buried with Christ. When Christ arose, that resurrection represented newness of life. The old, sinful life was forever done away with.

Everyone who believes in Jesus Christ now takes on that new, eternal life, and can never again come under God's judgment on sin. This is what is meant by the term "born again." God sees those who are "born again" as perfect again, like we were before the Fall in the Garden of Eden. Those who have not accepted Christ's death, burial, and resurrection as payment for their sin, however, must still face God's judgment during the Tribulation. Although all who enter the

Being saved through Jesus Christ's death, burial, and resurrection comes to an individual lost in sin when that person accepts God's free offer to redeem him or her. The Bible says simply: "Believe on the Lord Jesus Christ, and you will be saved" (Acts 16:31). A person must accept this gift of salvation; God doesn't force it on people.

There is no other way to be saved. Acts 4:12 says: "Nor is there salvation in any other, for there is no other name under heaven given among men by which we must be saved." And Jesus, himself, said, "I am the way, the truth, and the life. No one comes to the Father except through me" (John 14:6).

Tribulation will be lost (unsaved), millions will accept Christ for their salvation during that time.

REVEALING CHRIST

Revelation, the book in the Bible that most specifically presents prophecies covering the future, is another word for "apocalypse" or "unveiling." So, the Tribulation or Apocalypse is the revealing or unveiling of something. Actually it is the revealing of Jesus Christ in His full glory, majesty, and power when He returns to put an end to Armageddon.

Jesus, who is God, came the first time as a humble baby, born in a stable. He will come the second time as the King of all kings to set up an earthly reign for one thousand years, known as the Millennial Kingdom.

ON BEING "RAPTURE READY"

Paul the apostle says, speaking of all Christians, "For God did not appoint us to wrath, but to obtain salvation through our Lord Jesus Christ, who died for us, that whether we wake or sleep, we should live together with Him" (1 Thessalonians 5:9–10). In other words, the purpose of the Rapture is to keep God's children from the time of terror (*Find It Fast*: Revelation 3:10). They have simply believed in what Jesus did for them on the Cross. They are already clean in God's holy eyes. Christ's shed blood has cleansed them of all unrighteousness in the Father's view.

FIND
IT
FAST

WHEN HEAVEN'S RAPTURE ELEVATOR STOPS

What a Supper!

The Church, in God's eyes, is made up of all "born-again" believers (*Find It Fast:* John 3:3, 3:7). The Church is referred to as "the Bride of Christ" and Christians' union with Jesus is likened in the Bible to a marriage.

Jewish marriages were conducted under very strict conditions, and in specific traditional ways. That tradition is at the heart of how Christ and His relationship to His Church is arranged.

One Jewish custom has it that a marriage supper is arranged for the bride and groom. The Bible speaks of the "marriage supper of the Lamb" (*Find It Fast*: Revelation 19). We also read about the "Lamb of God, who takes away the sin of the world." "Lamb" is one of Christ's titles (*Find It Fast:* John 1:29).

The marriage supper of the Lamb, then, is an event that will follow the Rapture. Christ and His Church will go to the Father's house, where all believers will live forever with Him.

THE DATE SETTERS' DIARY

One logical question many Christians ask is: "When is Jesus Christ going to return?" There's nothing wrong with the question. God's children should look for Christ's return. However, when reading the Bible, we run across words like ". . . for you know neither the day nor the hour in which the Son of Man is coming" (Matthew 25:13).

We also read, "Watch therefore, for you do not know what hour your Lord is coming" (Matthew 24:42).

We understand that to mean "You're not going to know until I come for you."

However, many people throughout history have read those same words of Jesus and have come up with different interpretations than what He intended. They've somehow managed to get around all restrictions against precise date setting. So date setters keep trying and they also keep failing.

On a number of occasions, this date setting has created pure havoc. The following list includes some past failed attempts to pin a date to the Rapture and some dates that have yet to be proven wrong.

✠ A.D. 53

There was talk that Christ's return had already taken place, even before all the books of the Bible were written. The Thessalonians panicked when they heard a rumor that the day of the Lord was at hand, and they had missed the Rapture.

✠ 500

A Roman priest living in the second century predicted Christ would return in A.D. 500, based on the dimensions of Noah's ark.

✠ 1000

This year goes down as one of the most heightened periods of hysteria over the return of Christ. All members of society seemed affected by the prediction that Jesus was coming back at the start of the new millennium. No events like those prophesied by the Bible for the Endtime were transpiring at that time in history. The magical number

1000 was the sole reason for the expectation. During the concluding months of A.D. 999, all people were on their best behavior. Many sold their worldly goods and gave them to the poor, and swarms of pilgrims headed east to meet the Lord at Jerusalem. Buildings went unprepared, crops were left unplanted, and criminals were set free from jails.

✠ 1033

This year was cited as the beginning of the millennium because it marked one thousand years since Christ's crucifixion.

✠ 1524–1526

Muntzer, a leader of German peasants, announced that the return of Christ was near. He proclaimed that after he and his men destroyed the high and mighty, the Lord would return. This belief led to an uneven battle with government troops where he was strategically outnumbered. Muntzer claimed to have a vision from God where the Lord promised that He would catch the cannonballs of the enemy in the sleeves of his cloak. The vision proved false when Muntzer and his followers were mowed down by cannon fire.

✠ 1650–1660

The Fifth Monarchy Men looked for Jesus to establish a theocracy. They took up arms and tried to seize England by force. The movement died when the British monarchy was restored in 1660.

✠ 1666

To the citizens of London, 1666 was not a banner year. A bubonic plague outbreak killed a hundred thousand and the Great Fire of London struck the same year. The world seemed at an end to most

Londoners. The fact that the year ended with part of the Beast's number (666) didn't help matters either.

✠ 1809

Mary Bateman, who specialized in fortune-telling, had a magic chicken that laid eggs with end-time messages on them. One message said that Christ was coming. The uproar she created ended when she was caught, by an unannounced visitor, forcing an egg into the hen's oviduct. Mary was later hanged for poisoning a wealthy client. History does not record if the offended chicken attended the hanging.

✠ 1814

Spiritualist Joanna Southcott boldly announced she, by virgin birth, would produce the second Jesus Christ. When her abdomen began to swell, she naturally attracted a great deal of interest. Southcott died without giving birth. An autopsy revealed it had been a false pregnancy.

✠ 1836

John Wesley wrote that "the time, times and half a time" of Revelation 12:14 were 1058–1836, "when Christ should come" (A. M. Morris, *The Prophecies Unveiled*).

✠ 1843–1844

William Miller was the founder of an end-times movement that was so prominent it received its own name: Millerism. From his studies of the Bible, Miller determined that the Second Coming would happen sometime between 1843 and 1844. A spectacular meteor shower in 1833 gave the movement a good push forward. The buildup of anticipation continued until March 21, 1844, when Miller's one-year timetable ran out. Some followers set another date of October 22, 1844. This, too, failed, collapsing the movement. One follower described the days after the failed predictions: "The world made merry over the old Prophet's predicament. The taunts and jeers of the 'scoffers' were well-nigh unbearable" (*Days of Delusion—A Strange Bit of History* by Clara Endicott Sears, Houghton Mifflin).

✠ 1910

The revisit of Halley's comet was, for many, an indication of the Lord's Second Coming. The Earth actually passed through the gaseous tail of the comet. One enterprising man sold comet pills to people for protection against the effects of the toxic gases.

✠ 1914

Charles Russell, after being exposed to the teachings of William Miller, founded his own organization that evolved into becoming the Jehovah's Witnesses. In 1914, Russell predicted the return of Jesus Christ.

✠ 1918

In 1918, new math didn't help Charles Russell from striking out again.

✠ 1925

The Witnesses had no better luck in 1925. They already possessed the title of "Most Wrong Predictions." They would expand upon it in the years to come.

✠ 1967

When the city of Jerusalem was reclaimed by the Jews in 1967, prophecy watchers declared that the "Time of the Gentiles" had come to an end.

✠ 1973

A comet that turned out to be a visual disappointment nonetheless compelled one preacher to announce that it would be a sign of the Lord's return.

✠ 1975

The Jehovah's Witnesses were back at it in 1975. The failure of the forecast did not affect the growth of the movement. The *Watchtower* magazine, a major Witness periodical, has over 13 million subscribers.

✠ 1977

We all remember the killer bee scare of the late 1970s. One prophecy prognosticator linked the bees to Revelation 9:3–12. After twenty years of progression, the bees are still in Texas. We're beginning to think of them as the killer snails.

✠ 1982

A group called the Tara Centers placed full-page advertisements in many major newspapers for the weekend of April 24–25, 1982, announcing: "The Christ is Now Here!" They predicted that He was to make himself known "within the next two months." After the date passed, they said that the delay was only because the "consciousness of the human race was not quite right . . ." Boy, all these years and we're still not ready.

✜ 1984

The Jehovah's Witnesses made sure, in 1984, that no one else would be able to top their record of most wrong doomsday predictions. The Witnesses' record currently holds at nine. The years are: 1874, 1878, 1881, 1910, 1914, 1918, 1925, 1975, and 1984. Lately, the JWs are claiming they're out of the prediction business, but it's hard to teach an old dog new tricks. They'll be back.

✜ 1988

The book *88 Reasons Why the Rapture Is in 1988* came out only a few months before the event was to take place. What little time the book had, it used effectively. By the time September 11–13 rolled around, whole churches were caught up in the excitement the book generated. Some people were measuring themselves for wings. Finally, the days of destiny dawned and then set. No Jesus. The environment was not the same as Miller's 1844 failure. Surprisingly, the taunting by the unsaved was very brief. Although the time for the Rapture had been a three-day window from September 11 to 13, many gave up hope on the morning of the 12th.

✜ 1989

After the passing of the deadline in *88 Reasons,* the author of that book, Edgar Whisenant, came out with a new book called *89 Reasons Why the Rapture Is in 1989.* This book sold only a fraction of the number of his prior release.

✜ 1991

Menachem Schneerson, a Russian-born rabbi, called for the Messiah to come by September 9, 1991, the start of the Jewish New Year.

✠ 1992

A Korean group called Mission for the Coming Days had the Korea Church in an uproar in the fall of 1992. They foresaw October 28, 1992, as the date for the Rapture. Numerology was the basis for the date. Several camera shots that left ghostly images on pictures were thought to be a supernatural confirmation of the date.

✠ 1993

If the year 2000 was the end of the six-thousand-year cycle, then the Rapture should have taken place in 1993, because seven years are essential for the Tribulation to run its course. This was the thinking of a number of prophecy writers.

✠ 1994

Harold Camping in his book *Are You Ready?* predicted the Lord's return in September 1994. The book was full of numerology that added up to 1994 as the date of Christ's return.

✠ 1994

After promising they would not make any more end-time predictions, the Jehovah's Witnesses fell off the wagon and proclaimed 1994 as the conclusion of an eighty-year generation—the year 1914 had been the starting point.

✠ 1996

This year had a special month, according to one author. He foresaw the month of September as the time for our Lord's return. The Church Age should last two thousand years from the time of Christ's birth in 4 B.C.—that was his theory.

✠ 1996

California psychic Sheldon Nidle predicted the end would come when 16 million spaceships converged upon the Earth on December 17, 1996, along with a host of angels. Nidle explained the passing of the date by claiming the angels placed us in a holographic projection to preserve us and give us a second chance.

✠ 1997

Monte Judah looked for the Tribulation to start in February or March based on numerology and the Psalms: "I am preparing and warning others that the Great Tribulation spoken of by Daniel and Yeshua will begin February/March of 1997." Judah actually protested being listed as a date setter. He claimed he was being misrepresented, but his own words condemn him: "If what I say does not happen, then brand me as a false prophet, listen to me no more, and heap the ridicule on to prevent others from making the same mistake" (Monte Judah in the February 1996 *Yavoh* newsletter, published by Lion and Lamb Ministries).

✠ 1997

When Rabin and Arafat signed their peace pact on the White House lawn on September 13, 1993, some saw the events as the beginning of Tribulation. With the signing of the peace agreement, Daniel's 1260-day countdown was underway. By adding 1260 days to September 13, 1993, you get February 24, 1997.

✠ 1997

Stan Johnson of the Prophecy Club saw a "90 percent" chance that the Tribulation would start September 12, 1997. He based his conclusion on several end-time signs. The date of September 12 was chosen by Johnson because it would be Jesus' two thousandth birthday and it would also be the Day of Atonement, although not what is currently the Jewish Day of Atonement. Further supporting evidence came from Romanian pastor Dumitru Duduman. In several heavenly visions, Dumitru claimed to have seen the book of life. In one of his earlier visions, there were several pages yet to be completed. In his last vision, he noticed the book only had one page left. Doing some rough calculating, Johnson and friends figured the latest time frame for the completion of the book would have to be September 1997.

✠ 1998

Numerology: Because 666 times three equals 1998, some people pointed to this year as being a prophetically significant year.

✠ 1998

A Taiwanese cult operating out of Garland, Texas, predicted Christ would return on March 31, 1998. The group's leader, Heng-ming Chen, announced God would return and then invite the cult members aboard a UFO. The group abandoned their Second Coming prediction when a precursor event failed to take place. The cult's leader said God would appear on every channel 18 of every television in the world. Maybe God realized at the last minute that the Playboy Network was channel 18 on several cable systems, and He didn't want to have Christians watching a porn channel (*The New York Times* 3/4/98).

✠ 1998

Marilyn Agee in her book *The End of the Age* had her sights set on May 31, 1998. This date was to conclude the six-thousand-year cycle from the time of Adam. Agee looked for the Rapture to take place on Pentecost, also known as the feast of weeks. Another indicator was the fact that the Holy Spirit did not descend upon the apostles until fifty days from Christ's resurrection. Israel was born in 1948. Add the fifty days as years and you come up with 1998. After her May 31 Rapture date failed, Agee, unable to face up to her error, continued her date setting by using various Scripture references to point to June 7, 14, 21, and about ten other dates.

✠ 1999

Well, you can't call Marilyn Agee a quitter. After bombing out badly several times in 1998, Marilyn set a new date for the Rapture: May 21 or 22, 1999.

✠ 1999

Philip Berg, a rabbi at the Kabbalah Learning Center, New York, proclaimed that the end might arrive on September 11, 1999, when "a ball of fire will descend, destroying almost all of mankind, all vegetation, all forms of life."

✠ 2000

Numerology: If you divide 2000 by 3, you will get the devil's number 666.66666666666667.

✠ 2000

The list of names of people and organizations that called for the return of Christ at the turn of the century is too long to be listed here. We would say that if there was a day that Christ could not have come back, it would have been January 1, 2000. To come at an unknown time means an unknown time. January 2, 2000, would have been a more likely day for Him to call His Church home—right after the big letdown.

✠ 2002

Priests from Cuba's Afro-Caribbean Yoruba religion predicted a dramatic year of tragedy and crisis for the world in 2002, ranging from coups and war to disease and flooding.

✠ 2004

This date for Jesus' return is based upon Psalmology, numerology, the biblical 360 days per year, Jewish holidays, and "Biblical astronomy." To figure out this date, you'll need a calculator, a slide rule, and plenty of scratch paper.

✠ 2012

New Age writers cite Mayan and Aztec calendars that predict the end of the age on December 21, 2012.

Date Setters' Dilemma

An untold number of people have tried to predict the Lord's return by using elaborate timetables. Most date setters do not realize mankind has not kept an unwavering record of time. Anyone wanting to chart, for example, 100 B.C. to A.D. 2000 would have to contend with the fact that 46 B.C. was 445 days long, there was no year 0 B.C., and in 1582 we switched from Julian Years (360 days) to Gregorian (365 days). Because most prognosticators are not aware of all of these errors, their math is immediately off by several years.

We believe we will never know the exact day of Christ's return for His Church. It is God's nature to act independently from man's thinking. If He returned on a date that someone had figured out, that person would deprive God of His triumph. When it comes to His glory, God doesn't share the spotlight with anyone.

The return of Jesus Christ will easily be the most important event in history. The glory of Heaven contrasted with our lives on Earth is like comparing the job of running a hot dog stand with the job of President of the United States.

When it comes to knowing the *general* time frame of Christ's return for His Church, the Word of God is generous. As we saw in Chapter 1, Jesus forewarned us of a number of events that will take place. When we see the predicted events coming together, we can conclude that time is short. Most of the prophesied events will take place during the Tribulation. Any forewarning of their arrival would make the Rapture all the more likely, because it occurs at the start of the Tribulation. Our world today seems to be in that time frame. Don't miss that elevator!

END-TIME AILMENTS AND RAPTURE-READY RX

Date Setters' Syndrome People who come down with date setters' syndrome will typically attempt to predict the exact date that Jesus Christ will return. Of all the ailments and conditions, this one has a history of being the most contagious.

Symptoms Sufferers may have a history of setting several dates that have passed uneventfully. They are always looking for the mathematical significance of numbers found in the Bible.

Treatment Several Scriptures can be used to treat date setters, for example: "But of that day and hour no one knows, not even the angels of heaven, but My Father only" (Matthew 24:36) and "It is not for you to know times or seasons which the Father has put in His own authority" (Acts 1:7).

GET RAPTURED
OR
GET CAPTURED!

CHAPTER 3

Pre-Tribulation Rapture 101

"Hello," came the pleasant voice of the pastor Rayford had met several times.

As he spoke he sat on the edge of the desk in the very office Rayford had just visited.

"My name is Vernon Billings, and I'm pastor of the New Hope Village Church of Mount Prospect, Illinois. As you watch this tape, I can only imagine the fear and despair you face, for this is being recorded for viewing only after the disappearance of God's people from the earth.

. . . "Every person who believed in and accepted the sacrificial death, burial and resurrection of Jesus Christ anticipated his coming again for them. As you see this tape, all those will have already seen the fulfillment of the promise of Christ, when he said, 'I will come again and receive you unto myself, that where I am, there you may be also.'

. . . "Depending on when you're viewing this tape, you

may have already found that martial law is in effect in many places, emergency measures trying to keep evil elements from looting and fighting over the spoils of what is left. Governments will tumble and there will be international disorder.

. . . "I believe the Bible teaches that the Rapture of the church ushers in a seven-year period of trial and tribulation, during which terrible things will happen."

. . . Rayford paused the tape. He had been prepared for the salvation stuff. But tribulation and trial? Losing his loved ones, facing the pride and self-centeredness that had kept him out of heaven—wasn't that enough? There would be *more*?

—*Left Behind*

Rayford Steele, the 747 pilot in *Left Behind,* seeks an education in what the Rapture was all about. For him, and the others left behind, it's too late to avoid the Tribulation. The preacher gives him a quick videotaped Rapture/Tribulation 101 lecture after the fact. Millions have vanished. Next will come the horrors prophesied by Jesus and the Old and New Testament prophets. The most vicious dictator the world has ever known will soon begin his conquest of Planet Earth. All Jewish people, and people who will become Christians, will soon face capture and death by the beast and his regime.

We hope, with *Are You Rapture Ready?*, to present such a course before the fact, so you will know what to expect before, not after, the phenomenal event happens. This chapter is devoted to giving a Bible-based overview of why the Rapture will occur before the seven years of Tribulation begin. Armed with the information you need, you can then determine for yourself whether it's a good idea to be Rapture ready.

ALL IN THE FAMILY

Not all people who say that the concept of Rapture is insane come from the ranks of those who are not Christians. Many who claim Christianity as their religious home think the Rapture "theory" is just plain nuts.

Although we will address their most obvious arguments, we won't get into a shoving match with those folks here. We will, for the most part, instead confine our debate to squabbling with "the family." The family here being defined as those who accept the biblical truth that the Rapture will, in fact, occur. This is not to imply that we believe those who do not accept the Rapture theory are not Christians.

Rapture Ruckus

No other doctrinal issues bring about more uproar in the Christian ranks than do differences in belief about the Rapture. Many arguments over that event divide Christians who otherwise agree almost right down the line on crucial doctrines, such as those involving salvation. The whole debate comes down to a matter of the timing of the Rapture. When will it happen in relation to the Tribulation? That's the hang-up.

TRIBULATION TIMING

The great debate on the Rapture of the Church revolves around the Rapture's position—time wise—relative to the Tribulation era.

There are three basic positions:

1. the Pre-Tribulation position
2. the Mid-Tribulation position
3. the Post-Tribulation position

1. Pre-Tribulation Rapture

FIND
IT
FAST

This position puts forward the belief that the Rapture of the Church (all born-again believers in Jesus Christ as Savior) will be taken from Earth before the Tribulation begins. The view holds that all seven years of the Tribulation era are under God's judgment, and that Christians of the Church Age are not to endure God's wrath (*Find It Fast:* 1 Thessalonians 5: 9–10).

2. Mid-Tribulation Rapture

This is the belief that all Christians will be taken from Earth sometime around the middle of the Tribulation. This view holds that God's judgment doesn't begin to fall upon the planet until three and a half years of the Tribulation have passed.

3. Post-Tribulation Rapture

This viewpoint says that Christians will have to go through the entire seven years of the Tribulation era. The Rapture of the Church will then occur and Christians will join Jesus, who's then on His way back to put a stop to Armageddon.

Rapture Theories

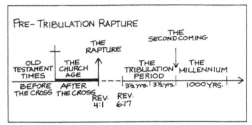

Pre-Tribulation Rapture
The church is raptured before the Tribulation period.

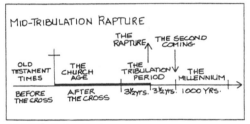

Mid-Tribulation Rapture
The church is raptured in the middle of the
Tribulation period.

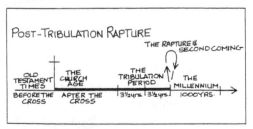

Post-Tribulation Rapture
The church is raptured after the Tribulation period.

Images from *Prophecy at Ground Zero: From Today's Mideast Madness
to the Second Coming of Christ,* William T. James, Ed. Courtesy of
Starburst Publishers, Lancaster, PA.

PRE-TRIB SIMPLY MAKES SENSE

We are convinced that the Bible teaches a Pre-Tribulation Rapture. It is, in the final analysis, the only position that brings all points of prophecy into account in the matter of the timing of the Rapture. Put more simply, it's the only position that makes sense. Jesus will come for the Church before the Tribulation begins.

The Unknown Hour

When we search the Scriptures and read the passages describing the Lord Jesus' return, we find verses that tell us we won't know the day and hour. At the same time, however, we find passages that give the precise number of days to look for regarding Christ's return. Is the Bible contradicting itself?

FIND IT FAST

Jesus himself said no man will know the day or hour. He says in Matthew 25:13 that He will return at an unknown time, while Revelation 12:6 indicates that the Jews will have to wait on the Lord 1,260 days from the time of a specific occurrence. Prophecy plainly teaches that the 1,260 days start when the Antichrist stands in the Temple of God and declares himself to be God: "[He] . . . exalts himself above all that is called God or that is worshiped, so that he sits as God in the temple of God, showing himself that he is God" (2 Thessalonians 2:4). This event will take place at the midpoint of the Tribulation (*Find It Fast*: Daniel 9:27).

It should be noted that some people see only a three-and-a-half-year Tribulation. They are in a way correct, because the first half of the Tribulation will be relatively peaceful compared to the second half. Peaceful or not, Bible prophecy teaches that this will be a full seven-year time period called the Tribulation.

GOD'S TWO PLANS OF ACTION

God, the Scriptures teach, has two distinct prophetic programs in the matter of dealing with human history and the end time. One is for the Church and the other is for the nation of Israel. You must separate these two agendas, or else prophecy about the Rapture makes no sense. Those who say the pre-Tribulation viewpoint is wrong, or who hold there is no Rapture at all, don't separate the two programs that are so plainly given in Scripture.

On the one hand, Jesus says that we cannot know the day or the hour when He comes. Paul and Peter say His coming will be a surprise. On the other hand, Jesus prophesied everybody would see Him returning, and that it will be possible for those who have become saved during the Tribulation to know exactly when He will return to Earth.

The Jews will know, when they are forced to flee into the wilderness in order to get away from Antichrist's blood-thirsty attempt to exterminate them, that all they have to do is hide in the place God has prepared for them, and wait out those 1,260 days (*Find It Fast:* Matthew 24:16).

FIND
IT
FAST

Many of those who scoff at a pre-Tribulation Rapture desperately try to make the point that Jesus' words "no man can know the hour or the day" of His coming have no relevance to a sudden, surprise coming. They argue that prophecy predicts that the time of Christ's coming can be determined exactly due to Israel's hiding in the place prepared for them by God, awaiting Messiah, who will come in 1,260 days. Certainly, Jesus' words can't just be ignored or thrown out. At the same time, there is no way that Christ's words about no man knowing the day or hour can apply to anything but a sudden, surprise coming. The only way these seemingly contradictory viewpoints—the sudden, unknown time of His coming, and His precisely given time of return—can be true is to separate the two distinct events. The Rapture of the Church comes before the Tribulation, and the return of Jesus to the Earth takes place at least seven years later. In other words, there are two distinct and separate phases to Christ's Second Coming.

What They Didn't Teach You in History Class

Many groups try to discredit the pre-Trib Rapture by saying most of the end-time events in the Bible have already taken place. A group of people called preterists claim that the book of Revelation was mostly fulfilled by A.D. 70. If the book of Revelation was past tense, we're at a loss to explain some of the current situations we see occurring around us: the rebirth of Israel, the reunification of Europe, the number of global wars that have occurred, and the development of nuclear weapons.

Asleep in Class?

FIND
IT
FAST

During history class, we must have slept through the part where the teacher talked about the time when a third of the trees were burned up, hundred-pound hailstones fell from the sky, and the sea turned into blood (*Find It Fast:* Revelation 8:7–8, 16:21). In our view, several people would have to question their opposition to the pre-Trib Rapture doctrine if they knew that the evidence provided to them was based on the premise that most Tribulation prophecies have already occurred.

Defending the Pre-Trib Rapture

After reading countless messages and articles that attack the pre-Trib Rapture, a certain number of arguments repeatedly surface. We will address those points of debate here.

1. **"Nowhere in the Bible does it directly say that the Church will be raptured before the Tribulation."**

   Pre-Trib opponents should have thought this one through because any pre-Tribulationst has the same right to say, "Nowhere in the Bible does it directly say the Church will go through the Tribulation." Jesus did say we should be ready because He will come when we least expect it (*Find It Fast:* Matthew 24:4). The only time frame we can think of during which believers would not be expecting Jesus to return would have to be before the Tribulation.

2. **The Margaret MacDonald Origin**

   One of the most widely circulated attacks against the pre-Trib Rapture is the notion that a girl named Margaret MacDonald started this theological view back in 1830. The claim is typically made that MacDonald received a demonic vision and passed it on to John Darby, a Christian scholar and theologian who in turn popularized it.

   FIND IT FAST

   Disproving this assertion proves rather easy. Pre-Trib scholars have discovered a host of Rapture writings that predated Margaret MacDonald. For example, Ephraem the Syrian said, in A.D. 373, "For all the saints and Elect of God are gathered, prior to the tribulation that is to come, and are taken to the Lord lest they see the confusion that is to overwhelm the world because of our sins."

One Post-Trib author offered a reward to anyone who could find a quote that predated MacDonald. He had to quickly cough up the money when someone identified a scholar who wrote about the Pre-Trib Rapture several years before MacDonald. As of late, dozens of examples have been found, and the literary surface has hardly been scratched.

With the revealing of all these pre-MacDonald writings, you would think that this argument has been debunked. Unfortunately, this is not the case. We seem to be involved in a tug-of-war with the truth. Apparently, due to their lack of research, Pre-Trib opponents continue to pump out publications that cite MacDonald as the originator of the Pre-Trib Rapture.

MARGARET MACDONALD WHO?

Margaret MacDonald, despite the false claims to the contrary, is not the mother of the Pre-Tribulation Rapture.

We have visited just about every Web site there is that is anti-Rapture in nature. One common arguing point nearly every one of these sites uses to oppose the Pre-Tribulation doctrine is the claim that the Rapture theory was started by a Scottish girl named Margaret MacDonald. Many critics of the Rapture declare that Ms. MacDonald received her vision from demonic origins, which she then passed on to infect the Church.

MacDonald's Credit Turned Down

Admittedly being staunch Pre-Tribulationists, we find it impossible to find connection between Margaret MacDonald and our holding to the Rapture. We can't recall ever hearing Pre-Trib speakers say, "I believe in the Rapture because Margaret MacDonald told me so."

After reading and listening to a number of Web sites, books, and radio programs that promote the idea that Margaret MacDonald started Pre-Tribulationism, we looked into the matter.

To be certain that there was no oversight on our part, we searched through our libraries of prophecy books looking for references that cited Margaret MacDonald as the founder of the Rapture teaching. Our hunt for a Pre-Tribulation accreditation to MacDonald turned out to be a vain one. It was like looking for the cartoon character "Where's Waldo." Only in this case, there was no Waldo to be found.

If MacDonald was the founder of the Pre-Tribulation Rapture, as most anti-Rapture proponents say she is, then someone needs to explain why Rapturists have failed to give her credit. You would expect to find dozens of books that expound upon her every word. From reading the writings of anti-Rapture authors, one would think we Pre-Tribbers should pay great homage to MacDonald. The lack of recognition being paid to MacDonald by Rapture believers is like a situation where the modern Mormon church failed to recognize Joseph Smith as their founder or today's Jehovah's Witnesses neglected to identify Charles Russell as their originator. Poor Margaret MacDonald, she gets all of the blame, but none of the credit.

After having examined the claims of those critical of the Rapture, we have found holes in their so-called evidence big enough to drive a dump truck through.

The first problem with the claim of the MacDonald origin is the fact that she wasn't the one who widely taught the doctrine of the Pre-Trib Rapture. A man named John Darby is believed by many to be the one who started the modern interest in the Rapture.

Truth about Darby

The question here is how did Darby come to hear of MacDonald's vision? Proponents of the claim that MacDonald founded the "Rapture theory," like Dave MacPherson and John L. Bray, have never been able to prove that Darby ever heard of MacDonald or her vision. Darby himself claims the revelation of the Rapture came to him when he realized the distinction between Israel and the Church.

Darby reported that he discovered the Rapture teaching in 1827, three years before MacDonald had her vision. When one closely examines MacDonald's vision, it becomes clear that her vision could not have been a Pre-Tribulation one. MacDonald looked for a "fiery trial which is to try us," and she foresaw the Church being purged by the Antichrist. Any Pre-Tribulation rapturist can tell you the Church will be removed before the advent of the Antichrist.

John Bray, an anti-Rapturist, said himself that Margaret Mac-Donald was teaching a single coming of our Lord Jesus. This con-tradicts current Rapture doctrine that teaches a two-staged event—Christ first coming for His Church and then, seven years later, His return to Earth. With so many contradictions between

MacDonald's vision and today's Pre-Tribulationism, we find it very difficult to see any linkage here.

Bray's Bad Gamble

By far the biggest mistake Post-Tribulationists have made in their attacks on the Rapture is their claim that the Pre-Tribulation Rapture was never taught before 1830. In fact, John L. Bray, a Southern Baptist evangelist, offered $500 to anyone who could prove that someone taught the Rapture doctrine prior to MacDonald's 1830 vision. John Bray was first proven wrong when in a newsletter, he wrote, "Then my own research indicated that it was Emmanuel Lacunza, a Jesuit Catholic priest, who in the 1812 book *The Coming of Messiah in Glory and Majesty,* first taught this theory." Bray stuck his neck out again when he made another $500 offer to anyone who could provide a documented statement earlier than Lacunza's 1812 writings. Well, apparently he had to fork over the five hundred bucks. We quote him again: "I offered $500 to anyone who would give a documented statement earlier than Lacunza's time which taught a two-stage coming of Christ separated by a stated period of time." No one ever rightfully claimed that $500 offer until someone found writings that forced Bray to write the following: "Now I have the Photostat copies of a book published in Philadelphia, Pennsylvania, in 1788 but written in 1742–1744 in England, which taught the pretribulation Rapture before Lacunza."

Pre-Trib Early Teachings

Lately, a number of other sources have been located that teach the Pre-Tribulation Rapture—some written as early as the second century. Now where does this leave Margaret MacDonald?

In our lives here on Earth, we've made a number of observations that we regard as undeniable truths. One of these is the fact that the truth will suffer attacks with no one defending it, while a lie will be allowed to proliferate with no one challenging it. This is what seems to have taken place in the case of the Rapture. For years on end, anti-Rapturists have been allowed to freely attack Pre-Tribulationism. One assailant called the Rapture the mark of the beast, while another remarked that when Jesus returns at the battle of Armageddon, He will fight against those who believe in the Rapture.

The men who should have been contending for the Rapture, have, for the most part, just sat there saying, "That may be your opinion." At last, it appears that those who hold to a Pre-Tribulation Rapture are starting to counter these ridiculous charges.

A number of books have been published that cite several pre-MacDonald sources that describe a Raptured Church. Author Grant Jeffrey deserves a good deal of the praise for his work in discovering many of these pre-MacDonald sources.

As far as being able to find the Pre-Tribulation Rapture in the Bible is concerned, we do not think anyone needs to be a nuclear physicist to discover it. We are unable to vouch for everyone else, but for us, locating the Rapture doctrine in the Bible is as simple as finding evidence that Jesus Christ is Messiah.

The evidence that Christians believed in the Rapture long before MacDonald does not seem to have sunk into the minds of those opposed to the Rapture. They still teach that she is the founder of Pre-Tribulationism. When people are presented with overwhelming proof that what they believed to be the truth is in fact wrong, and they refuse to accept that truth, then you certainly have to conclude that they are in spiritual darkness.

No evidence whatsoever points to MacDonald as the source of Pre-Tribulationism. Every major prophetic author alive today claims the Word of God as the foundation for believing in the Rapture. As discussed at length throughout this chapter and this book, both Jesus Christ and the Apostle Paul made statements that clearly establish the Rapture doctrine. Jesus said, in Matthew 25:13, "Watch therefore, for you know neither the day nor the hour in which the Son of Man is coming." Paul affirmed in 1 Thessalonians 4:16–18: "For the Lord Himself will descend from heaven with a shout, with the voice of an archangel, and with the trumpet of God. And the dead in Christ will rise first. Then we who are alive and remain shall be caught up together with them in the clouds to meet the Lord in the air. And thus we shall always be with the Lord. Therefore comfort one another with these words."

3. The Last Trumpet Argument

Because Paul said believers would be raptured at the sounding of a trump, many folks have tried to make it appear that the Rapture trumps are the same ones found in Revelation 11:15–18, Joel 2:1, and Matthew 24:31—which all occur during the Tribulation. When you have trumpets commonly used throughout the Bible, it's foolish to just assume any two of the sixty-two trumps or trumpets are prophetically related. To be able to make the claim that the Tribulation trumpet soundings are the same as the Rapture trumps, you would need a direct statement saying this is the case. In the movies *Ben-Hur* and *The Wizard of Oz*, we hear the sounding of trumpets. Are both these trumpets somehow prophetically related?

FIND IT FAST

If your friend John said he went to his favorite restaurant last night, and another friend Larry said he also went to his favorite restaurant last night, is it logical to assume they went to the same restaurant? Obviously not, because even though John and Larry went to their favorite restaurants, they may have had two different eating establishments in mind. The same logic should apply with the word "trumpet."

With such a blind devotion to this one similarity, we have to wonder if these last-trumpeters are able to distinguish the difference between Tylenol and Ex-Lax. They're both over-the-counter drugs, they come in pill form, and they can also be found in a medicine cabinet. Of course, one will make your headache disappear and the other will make your toilet paper disappear.

4. Pre-Wrath Presumptuousness

FIND
IT
FAST

Pre-wrath proponents say that the seventh trumpet blown in Revelation 11:15–18 is the same "last trump" Paul spoke of in 1 Corinthians 15:52. They, therefore, argue that the Pre-Tribulation Rapture is in error, since that last trump is scheduled as part of God's judgments deep into the Tribulation. That trumpet will be blown, they proclaim, at the beginning of the "Great Tribulation" Jesus referred to in Matthew 24:21. That trumpet blast, they say, initiates God's wrath and, subsequently, the Rapture. However, they fail to take into account the fact that John wrote Revelation forty years after Paul wrote his first letter to the Corinthians. How could Paul refer to something that was not yet revealed?

5. Post-Trib Trumpet Talk

Post-Tribbers use a trumpet sounding in Joel 2:1 as evidence for a Post-Trib Rapture on the Day of the Lord. We have three problems with Joel 2:1:

⊕ First, Joel clearly says that the purpose for blowing the trumpet is to "sound an alarm."

⊕ Second, according to 1 Corinthians 15:15, the Rapture takes place in an instant, and is a surprise occurrence. Joel 2:1 says the Day of the Lord is at hand. In order for Joel's trumpet to be the same one as in 1 Corinthians, there would have to be a time delay between the sounding of the trumpet and the Rapture of the Church.

⊕ Third, the fact that another trumpet is being sounded in Joel 2:15 further clouds the possibility that these trumpets could have anything to do with the Rapture. When Paul was writing to the Corinthians, he specifically said "the" last trump. During the Feast of Trumpets, the Jews blow short trumpet blasts. They end the feast with a long blast from what is called the last trump, which is blown the longest. Judaism has traditionally connected this last trump with the resurrection of the dead. Paul also made the connection. For many Christians, the association between the Rapture and the Feast of Trumpets is so strong, they look for the Rapture to someday occur on this feast.

6. The Day of the Lord Argument

A number of people have attempted to refute the Pre-Trib Rapture by trying to associate the "Day of the Lord" with a catching up of believers at the end of the Tribulation. They base their Rapture views solely on the idea that the "Day of

DAY OF THE LORD

Let's examine some verses that clearly indicate the term "day" is used to represent a broader time period.

⊕ **2 Peter 3:10–13** The "Day of the Lord" Peter spoke of in this instance cannot be a one-day event because it mentions the destruction of the Earth by fire and its renovation.

⊕ **Revelation 21:11** This passage tells us the Earth will not be renewed until after Christ's thousand-year reign.

⊕ **Joel 2:11–20** The "Day of the Lord" Joel describes includes the defeat of an army from the North. Ezekiel 38 and 39 are parallel passages. Most scholars time the destruction of the Gog army referred to here as occurring in the first half of the Tribulation.

⊕ **John 12:48** In the book of John, Jesus uses the term "last day" to indicate when the lost will be judged. Revelation 20 makes it clear that the unsaved will not be judged until after the Millennium—yet another thousand-year gap.

⊕ **Hebrews 10:25** One of the best indications that most of the various "day" references are citing a general time period can be found in Hebrews 10:25: "Not forsaking the assembling of ourselves together, as is the manner of some, but exhorting one another, and so much the more as you see the Day approaching." Surely, Paul would not be warning us to watch for a day that would be coming at the end of the Tribulation. That type of logic would be like warning children, as they cross the road, to watch out for taillights.

the Lord" and the Rapture are either synonymous or somehow linked together. The Achilles' heel of their argument has to be the notion that the "Day of the Lord" and various other "days" of an end-time context refer to a twenty-four-hour period that occurs at or near the end of the Tribulation. Probably the most commonly cited verse is 1 Thessalonians 5:2, in which Paul tells us the "Day of the Lord" will come "as a thief in the night."

Countless articles describe the "Day of the Lord" as Christ's advent at Armageddon. These articles go on to say that, because Paul also tells us the Lord will come "as a thief," we have a direct link to the same description that is applied to noted Rapture verses. It's rather obvious that those trying to rely on the "Day of the Lord" never bothered to validate the meaning of this particular day. Upon checking a number of commentaries on the "Day of the Lord," we find that many of them define this as being an all-encompassing period that begins with the Great Tribulation.

GOD CAN'T LIE

The Creator of all things cannot lie (*Find It Fast:* Titus 1:2). He inspired the Apostle Paul to write: "For the Lord himself shall descend from heaven with a shout, with the voice of the archangel, and with the trumpet of God. And the dead in Christ will rise first. Then we who are alive and remain shall be caught up together with them in the clouds to meet the Lord in the air. And thus we shall always be with the Lord" (1 Thessalonians 4: 16–17).

That's the Rapture!

God also inspired Paul to give Christians the marvelous promise: "For God did not appoint us to wrath, but to obtain salvation through our Lord Jesus Christ, who died for us, that whether we wake or sleep, we should live together with Him" (1 Thessalonians 5:9–10).

That's the *Pre-Tribulation* Rapture!

END-TIME AILMENTS AND RAPTURE-READY RX

Rapture Rabies A psychosomatic reaction that people have to the very mention of the Pre-Tribulation Rapture. People with RR have a mental dislike of the Pre-Trib view.

Symptoms The afflicted person's prophetic interest is exclusively centered on writings that discuss the timing of the Rapture. As a group, these folks are always seeking individuals who will agree with their viewpoint.

Treatment The realization that the Pre-Trib Rapture is an unknown event that must transpire ahead of the Tribulation is the best cure. "Watch therefore, for you know neither the day nor the hour in which the Son of Man is coming" (Matthew 25:13).

LOOK UP,
OR
LOOK OUT!

CHAPTER 4

Guilt-Free Escapism

Tel Aviv was choked with foot and vehicular traffic that led to the seashore and the great makeshift amphitheater that would house the mark application equipment. Everything was in place, including covered areas to blunt the brunt of the sun. All that was left to be installed were the injectors, the enforcement facilitators, and the personnel to man the site. People were already in line, eager to be among the first to pledge their loyalty to Nicolae . . . As he parked his rental several blocks from the site, Buck dreamed of abandoning reason and shouting to the uninformed, "Don't do it! You're selling your soul to the devil!"

. . . All Buck knew was that what he had endured in three and a half years was a walk in the park compared to what was coming . . .

Buck had never been fearful, never one to back down in the face of mortal danger. But Nicolae Carpathia was evil personified, and the next day Buck would be in the line of fire when the battle of the ages between good and evil for the very souls of men and women would burst from the heavens, and all hell would break loose on earth.

—Tim LaHaye and Jerry B. Jenkins, *The Mark*
(Wheaton, Illinois: Tyndale House, 2000)

THE MARK

The Mark, one of the novels of the *Left Behind* series, gives a glimpse into the prophesied time when the world dictator will be master of all he surveys. Well, not quite *all.*

Bible prophecy says a great host of people—probably many millions—will resist Antichrist and be murdered for their faith. These are a particular people whom the Antichrist and his henchmen will hunt down and massacre during the Tribulation.

John, apostle and prophet, recorded: "I saw under the altar the souls of those who had been slain for the word of God and for the testimony which they held. And they cried with a loud voice, saying, 'How long, O lord, holy and true, until you judge and avenge our blood on those who dwell on the earth?' Then a white robe was given to each of them; and it was said to them that they should rest a little while longer, until both the number of their fellow servants and their brethren, who would be killed as they were, was completed" (Revelation 6:9–11).

BELIEVERS ABOUND

There is no question that there will be many Christians living during that time of horrors. Most of them will die for their faith, the Bible says.

John, to whom the Revelation was given, wrote: "It was granted to him to make war with the saints and to overcome them. And authority was given him [Antichrist] over every tribe, tongue, and nation" (Revelation 13:7).

MANDATORY MARK

The novel *The Mark* accurately portrays Antichrist's forcing everybody to take a specific mark of allegiance to him or suffer the consequences. Again, John wrote: "He was granted power to give breath to the image of the beast, that the image of the beast should both speak and cause as many as would not worship the image of the beast to be killed. He causes all, both small and great, rich and poor, free and slave, to receive a mark on their right hand or on their foreheads, and that no one may buy or sell except one who has the mark or the name of the beast, or the number of his name" (Revelation 13:15–16).

Who Are These Saints?

Those who belong to Christ will refuse that mark, prophecy says. Who are these Christians, these "saints" who refuse the mark of the beast? That is the question.

That these saints are prominent in the Tribulation, according to the prophecies in the book of Revelation, is the main argument that some use against a Pre-Tribulation Rapture. The presence of believers, who die by the millions, is proof, the Rapture rippers say, that Christians will go through the Tribulation.

Fly-Away Accusations

The Rapture, particularly the Pre-Trib Rapture, is often called "pie-in-the-sky, in the sweet-bye-and-bye escapism" by those who believe the Church must go through the Tribulation, or a big part of that terrible time on Earth, in order to wash or cleanse themselves so they can be worthy to enter Heaven when it's all over.

Pre-Trib Rapture opponents attempt to lay a heavy guilt trip on those who believe there is a God-ordained escape from the time of Antichrist. Detractors apparently believe it should be within the nature of Christians to prefer the fires of wrath to the love and comfort of their Savior and God. They proclaim that prophecy says Antichrist will overcome the saints. This, they say, shows the Church is in the middle of the massacre by the beast's regime.

CHRIST REFUTES FALSE FATE

Jesus prophesied an entirely different fate for His Church. He said, ". . . and on this rock I will build my church, and the gates of Hades will not overcome it" (Matthew 16:18). This once and for all refutes the argument that Antichrist, Satan's man, will overcome Christ's Church. Since God's Word never contradicts itself, we can know that the Church cannot both go through the Tribulation and be "overcome" by Antichrist, and at the same time, receive this promise. It will absolutely never happen. We have God's Word on it.

CHRIST'S COMFORT CLEAR

The Bible tells the exact opposite of God's oppressive hand of judgment upon Christians of the Church Age. Paul, after prophesying the Rapture in 1 Thessalonians 4:13–17, says this: "Therefore comfort one another with these words" (1 Thessalonians 4:18).

FIND IT FAST

He says further, after telling Christians they are not appointed to wrath in 1 Thessalonians 5:9: "Therefore comfort each other and edify one another, just as you are also doing" (1 Thessalonians 5:11).

Nowhere is the Church of Jesus Christ told to fear Antichrist, or anyone or anything else in the coming Tribulation. That's because the Church won't be here on Earth at that time. Instead, Christians of the Church Age are to encourage each other with the promise that they are not going to have to endure God's wrath during the time of Tribulation.

Believers' Bail-Out

The late Dr. J. Vernon McGee, who hosted the *Thru the Bible* radio program, was fond of saying this about the Rapture: If he was in a burning building, he would run out the door, jump out a window, go up the chimney, or take any way he could find to get out of there. He then said there is only one way to escape the burning fire of the place God calls hell, and there's only one way to escape the hell of the coming Tribulation: Jesus Christ, who, himself, said, "I am the way, the truth, and the life. No one comes to the Father except through Me" (John 14:6).

DOORWAYS OUT OF DISASTER

Jesus Christ is called "the door" in a number of places in the Bible. The escape from the coming Tribulation for Christians has two doors. Each door, like a fire escape door marked with "EXIT," has "JESUS" on it. One door is death; the other is Rapture.

- ⊕ **Death's Door** People who have accepted Christ for the saving of their souls go directly into the Lord's presence when they die. The Apostle Paul wrote: "So we are always confident, knowing that while we are at home in the body we are absent from the Lord . . . We are confident, yes, well pleased rather to be absent from the body and to be present with the Lord" (2 Corinthians 5:6,8).
- ⊕ **Rapture's Door** People who are alive when Christ calls, "Come up here" (Revelation 4:1) will leave Planet Earth in a moment, in the "twinkling of an eye," via the Rapture. That's when, as Paul says in 1 Thessalonians 4:17, "we who are alive and remain shall be caught up together with them in the clouds to meet the Lord in the air. And thus we shall always be with the Lord" (1 Thessalonians 4:17).

The major point is this: God has provided a way to escape both eternal damnation and the coming time on Earth that will be by far the worst in human history. Whether it seems ludicrous, silly, impossible, or just plain

nuts makes no difference. God's Word promises that the Rapture
will occur before the Tribulation (*Find It Fast:* 1 Thessalonians 5:9).

ANTI-PRE-TRIBULATION RAPTURE ROCK THROWERS

Many groups of Christians oppose the Pre-Trib Rapture. These
people actually seem to look forward to the Tribulation. What else is
to be made of their adamant opposition to even the idea of escaping
that time of coming judgment? They view Pre-Tribulation Rapture
as being pure escapism.

Mid-Trib/Post-Trib Naysayers

The two main groups within Christianity that hold that there will
be a Rapture, or series of Raptures, but that the Pre-Tribulation position is escapism mumbo jumbo, are the Mid-Trib group and the
Post-Trib group.

The Mid-Tribulation group's position is more popularly known
these days as the "Pre-Wrath" position. This belief says that Christ

will remove Christians before God's wrath begins to fall on Earth. This, they propose, will take place at about three and one-half years into the seven-year Tribulation era. The Church (all Christians alive at the time) will have to go through the first three and one-half years, because the troubles that occur during that period are the wrath of man, not of God.

The Post-Tribulation position means just what its name implies: There is a Rapture scheduled, but it will occur after the entire Tribulation has run its course.

Earning a Tribulation Wage

Most Pre-Wrath and Post-Trib folks have the general idea that we need to somehow earn our way to Heaven by doing battle with the Antichrist. But, just as people can only go to Heaven by accepting what Jesus did on the cross, the only true way to obtain free passage to Heaven by means of the Rapture is through Jesus Christ. He has paid the ticket for that trip, just as He paid the debt for all sin with His death, burial, and resurrection. There is nothing anyone can do by his or her own efforts to get to Heaven, or to be kept out of Tribulation, or to get through the Tribulation.

Poor Prophecy Planning

The Tribulation saint wanna-bes crowd promotes a bold yet hollow message. Most are so busy attacking Pre-Tribulationism that they fail to lay out any practical advice for what Christians should do during the Tribulation. In fact, nearly all instruction, encouragement, and guidance offered to people who will find themselves on the wrong side of the Rapture have been produced by Pre-Trib authors.

Throwing Mud Balls

Visit any Post-Tribulation Web site, and you will generally find article after article detailing displeasure with the Pre-Trib view. Features with titles such as "Pre-Trib Hypocrisy," "LaHaye's Temperament," "An Open Letter to Todd Strandberg," and "Deceiving and Being Deceived" are all highly caustic, hate-filled documents. You would think these folks would be producing articles on wilderness survival or how to endure persecution rather than throwing mud balls that do nothing but splatter the Body of Christ in the eyes of the world.

Once the Rapture takes place, Web pages with titles like "Why Pre-Tribulation Rapture Doctrine Is False" will become instantly antiquated. One has to wonder about the type of confusion these articles will create for people who encounter them after the great event.

The devil will certainly take full advantage of the negative bombardment people have aimed at the Pre-Trib Rapture. It's quite likely that a common explanation for the mass disappearance of millions of Christians will be that God took the troublesome people away to be judged.

Disturbing Error

The most disturbing error regarding Post-Trib thinking is the belief that Christians are promised special protection from the Tribulation horrors. Some people try to use certain passages to claim God will protect Christians, but most of them use their own logic to conclude God's grace will allow us to stay perfectly safe those seven long years.

The Bible repeatedly states that Tribulation saints will face the strong likelihood of being martyred under the Antichrist's demonic rule. Yet, many so-called scholars are able to read the following Scriptures and conclude that the passages only suggest that a mild level of persecution will occur during the Tribulation.

⊕ "It was granted to him to make war with the saints and to overcome them. And authority was given him over every tribe, tongue, and nation" (Revelation 13:7).

⊕ "He who leads into captivity shall go into captivity; he who kills with the sword must be killed with the sword. Here is the patience and faith of the saints" (Revelation 13:10).

⊕ "He was granted power to give breath to the image of the beast, that the image of the beast should both speak and cause as many as would not worship the image of the beast to be killed" (Revelation 13:15).

⊕ "Here is the patience of the saints; here are those who keep the commandments of God and the faith of Jesus. Then I heard a voice from heaven saying to me, 'Write: "Blessed are the dead who die in the Lord from now on"'" (Revelation 14:12–13).

⊕ "And I saw thrones, and they sat on them, and judgment was committed to them. Then I saw the souls of those who had been beheaded for their witness to Jesus and for the word of God, who had not worshiped the beast or his image, and had not received his mark on their foreheads or on their hands. And they lived and reigned with Christ for a thousand years" (Revelation 20:4).

ZECHARIAH 13:8–9

Two-thirds of the people of Israel will die during the Tribulation. The remaining one-third will go safely through the Tribulation era, protected by God, and will be the remnant that will make up the nation in its final form. The Lord will use the seven-year span to bring national salvation to Israel.

HOLOCAUST II

The Tribulation period is going to be equally bad for the Jews. The nation of Israel will suffer a horrendous amount of persecution. The prophet Zechariah predicts two-thirds of the Jewish people will perish. If 66 percent of Israel is wiped out, where does that leave the Gentile Christians?

Unaware World

The folks in the "unsaved" camp disapprove of the Pre-Trib Rapture because it implies the destruction of their world. Most unbelievers are unaware of what the end times imply. They would gladly bid good riddance to those annoying Christians who are always trying to "save their souls."

The few individuals who have gained enough knowledge of Bible prophecy to realize that the Rapture would, if true, herald global calamity, are generally displeased with Rapture-happy Christians. They have uneasy suspicions that believers in Christ just might escape off to Heaven while the world erupts into chaos.

Misdirected Malice

There is no need for unsaved folks to get irate with prophecy-minded Christians. God, not His children, is the director of all end-time events. The fact that He boldly takes credit for everything that occurs during the Tribulation doesn't leave much room for argument. Those who are angry with end-time talk and Rapture rhetoric should blame Him, not Christian neighbors and acquaintances.

On the other hand, it might be wise to reconsider blaming God. Only a fool would try to dispute the Almighty. The best advice anyone could give is for everyone to follow God's plan—it's the best one we'll find.

As Good as Advertised, or Even Better!

An old saying goes, "If it sounds too good to be true, then it probably is." This rule can never be applied to the Rapture, because the vast majority of people don't realize the Rapture is such a great deal. To be included in the "blessed hope" of Titus 2:13, a person must fulfill the same simple requirement for salvation: faith in Christ. "Jesus answered and said to him, 'Most assuredly, I say to you, unless one is born again, he cannot see the kingdom of God' " (John 3:3).

ONE RAPTURE-READY REQUIREMENT

There is no twelve-step program that people need to graduate from, nor is there a list of good works that must be accomplished, before one is truly Rapture ready. But nonetheless, most people will miss the Rapture. What truly makes the Rapture "guilt-free escapism" is the fact that everyone who misses out will do so out of his or her own neglect. In other words, those who are raptured shouldn't feel guilty that they miss the wrath of God. It's not their fault that those who are left behind refuse to accept Christ, and thereby fail to be Rapture ready.

If you were to poll people after the Rapture regarding why they were left behind, you'd probably hear a lot of weak responses. People will likely say things like "I was too busy for religion," "I was going to wait until I got older," "I had a bad experience with some so-called believers," or "my parents tried to force me to attend church." No one will be able to claim, "I tried to become a Christian, but God rejected my application."

Just Trust

All who will be caught up in the Rapture will be granted the privilege solely because they trusted in Jesus Christ as their Savior. It is quite interesting how the salvation issue, both before and after the Rapture, is so well balanced. Before the Rapture, people must exercise faith to overcome the lack of visible, physical evidence that God is at work in the world. After the Rapture, there will be plenty of physical evidence that God works in the affairs of man, but then a person will need great faith to overcome the trials of the Tribulation.

Holy Help

Most Christians are totally unaware of how involved the Holy Spirit is in the world. The Holy Spirit

- ⊕ puts in our minds the need for God
- ⊕ makes the world conscious of its sin
- ⊕ strengthens faith of believers
- ⊕ convinces that God's prophetic Word is truth
- ⊕ is a direct line of communication between God and man

The total impact of God the Holy Spirit is restraint upon the evil in the world.

Many scholars believe that "He" in the following passage refers to the Holy Spirit. That means the Holy Spirit, who is currently holding back wickedness in the world, will be removed during the Rapture: "For the mystery of lawlessness is already at work; only He who now restrains will do so until He is taken out of the way. And then the lawless one will be revealed. Whom the Lord will consume with the breath of His mouth and destroy with the brightness of His coming" (2 Thessalonians 2:7–8). The Holy Spirit's departure from Earth is what will allow the Antichrist to set up the great deception.

Unholy Hindrance

Before the day of Pentecost, when the Holy Spirit entered living believers, evil spirits had the ability to possess and influence people more directly than they do today. The removal of the Holy Spirit's restraining ministry will probably be a reversal of the outpouring of miraculous signs and wonders described in the second chapter of Acts. Once the Rapture takes place, demonic activity will likely surpass the levels seen during the Old Testament times.

Some Will See

At the same time great deception pervades the Earth's population, keeping people from coming to Christ for salvation, many people will spiritually see the truth. When the supernatural catching up of the Church transpires, many barriers that had hindered people from believing in Christ will instantly vanish. People who previously thought the Bible was full of contradictions, errors, unanswered questions, and unproven theories will have solid proof the Word of God is true. It is hard to imagine how anyone in his right mind in a post-Rapture world could still hold to an atheistic, agnostic, or Darwinian view.

Some Will Suffer

Those who refuse to accept Christ before the Rapture occurs will be left behind. They will then have to choose Christ for salvation or accept Antichrist's mark. To accept Christ during the Tribulation means the believer will most likely be martyred because of his faith.

SATAN'S SUPERNATURAL SHOW

Satan will be manifesting some supernatural events of his own, particularly during the first half of the Tribulation. The devil will be free to empower the Antichrist to perform all sorts of miracles:

⊕ "For false christs and false prophets will rise and show great signs and wonders to deceive, if possible, even the elect" (Matthew 24:24).

⊕ "He performs great signs, so that he even makes fire come down from heaven on the earth in the sight of men. And he deceives those who dwell on the earth by those signs which he was granted to do in the sight of the beast, telling those who dwell on the earth to make an image to the beast who was wounded by the sword and lived" (Revelation 13:13–14).

YOUR RAPTURE-READY RELIANCE

For the non-Christian, there is still time this side of the Rapture to get ready to meet Christ when He calls. Nothing anyone says against the truth of a Pre-Tribulation Rapture should deter anyone in his or her decision.

Jesus is the only reliance for finding refuge from the catastrophic events of the Tribulation. He is the only one who can assure eternity spent with God, rather than eternity spent apart from God. Why not go with the option of accepting Christ before the Rapture? The decision is yours to make. Whatever you do, don't allow this wonderful opportunity to pass you by. "Watch therefore, and pray always that you may be counted worthy to escape all these things that will come to pass, and to stand before the Son of Man" (Luke 21:36).

For the Christian, there is no reason for feeling guilty about wanting to escape the coming apocalyptic events prophesied for the last seven years of human history that will precede Christ's Second Coming. Going through that time of hell on Earth for the Church Age Christian is not desirable, advantageous, or predicted by Bible prophecy. Rather, Jesus has promised: "If I go and prepare a place for you, I will come again and receive you to Myself; that where I am, there you may be also" (John 14:3).

END-TIME AILMENTS AND RAPTURE-READY RX

Obsessive-Compulsive Mark Disorder The Bible tells saints to avoid receiving a financial-related mark that will be issued by the Antichrist. Some individuals take this warning to an extreme level by viewing every system used for identification as being the "mark of the beast"—gym cards, Social Security numbers, license plates.

Symptoms People with OCMD will often have intense fixations with the beast number—666—and any number mathematically related to it. They have also been known to have a strong dislike of the color red.

Treatment Logical thinking is the best treatment for OCMD. People need to realize that the mark is a financial system that people will have to willingly accept. "He causes all, both small and great, rich and poor, free and slave, to receive a mark on their right hand or on their foreheads" (Revelation 13: 6).

THE
TERMINUS
IS PROXIMATE!

CHAPTER 5

Supercalifragilistic-
expealidociousism

For years he had tolerated church. They had gone to one that
demanded little and offered a lot. They made many friends
and had found their doctor, dentist, insurance man, and even
country club entrée in that church. Rayford was revered,
proudly introduced as a 747 captain to newcomers and
guests, and even served on the church board for several years.

When Irene discovered the Christian radio station and
what she called "real preaching and teaching," she grew dis-
enchanted with their church and began searching for a new
one. That gave Rayford the opportunity to quit going at all,
telling her that when she found one she really liked, he
would start going again. She found one, and he tried it
occasionally, but it was a little too literal and personal
and challenging for him. He was not revered. He felt like a
project. And he pretty much stayed away . . .

". . . Salvation." Another ten-dollar church word that

had never really impressed him. He knew Irene's new church was interested in the salvation of souls, something he'd never heard in the previous church. But the closer he had gotten to the concept, the more he had been repelled. Didn't salvation have something to do with confirmation, baptism, testifying, getting religion, being holy?

He hadn't wanted to deal with it, whatever it was. And, now he was desperate to know exactly what it meant.

—*Left Behind*

RELIGIOUS GOBBLEDYGOOK

Left Behind main character Rayford Steele's wife and son have vanished with the millions of others. He thumbs through the Bible he gave Irene on their first wedding anniversary. He remembers how much church had meant to his wife, and how little it had meant to him. He wishes he had paid more attention to what it was all about.

Too often, we regard religious matters and church membership as things we must endure, or as a way to meet people who can help us climb the social and business ladders. Through peer pressure to practice "do-goodism," we're often given only the "feel-goodisms" of politically and socially correct thought by nonjudgmental, compromising, modern preachers. God's message of salvation through Christ's sacrifice as payment for our sin is grossly neglected.

Like Rayford Steele, who was left behind because he was not "Rapture ready," most of us are receiving little of the true Gospel while we sit in church pews. The "real" preaching and teaching Rayford remembered his wife, Irene, talking about after she heard a Christian radio program are hard to come by. Although some ministers do continue to broadcast Gospel truth today, most media theologians speak in great, flowing words that either go over our heads or else appeal to our love of money and our lust for what it will buy. It is just religious gobbledygook.

When it comes to Christianity these days, we are living in the generation of supercalifragilisticexpealidociousism!

Mary Poppinsism

In the song "Supercalifragilisticexpialidocious" from the Disney film *Mary Poppins,* Dick Van Dyke and Julie Andrews sing these lyrics: "Even though the sound of it is something quite atrocious, if you say it loud enough, you'll always sound precocious..." This perfectly describes how many Christian leaders have distorted the original message Jesus commanded His disciples to preach.

Simply Put ...

When Jesus sent His disciples out into the world, He didn't leave them a mountain of instructions on how to operate the newly formed Christian religion. Nor did Jesus tell His disciples to develop a cumbersome system of religious jargon and ceremonies.

Instead, His command was very simple: He told His disciples to preach the "good news," the "glad tidings," and simply to be His "witnesses" (Acts 1:8).

FIND IT FAST

The Apostle Paul described the Gospel with equally simple language: He referred to the "blessed hope" in Titus 2:13, and in 1 Corinthians 1:23 he summed up his whole ministry in few words: to preach "Christ crucified."

Complex Competition

Thousands of other religions compete against Christianity in the world today. Very few of these can match the Gospel's simplicity. If you were to check into the salvation plan of some of these other religions, most would give a mumbo jumbo spiel like this: "To find the ultimate state of consciousness you need to achieve complete symmetry between the celestial and physical planes of existence."

Simple Salvation Sense

Most ministers simply fail to appreciate and respect the ignorance of their congregation when it comes to Bible truth. The preachers might have a degree from a well-respected seminary and they may have been studying the Bible for decades; yet they still may not have learned how to teach people the essentials of the Kingdom of God.

In social settings, it seems to be part of people's nature to pretend to understand difficult things, especially when they realize their comprehension is not going to be tested. They want to avoid feeling foolish because of their ignorance. This is a primary reason many churches are full of people who are totally without knowledge of the Word of God.

Ignorance Analogy

The home Web site for this book is Rapture Ready. Its Internet address is obviously www.raptureready.com. Nearly all Web search engines keep track of the words that people use to find the site. Most people who come to Rapture Ready find it by using the words "rapture" or "prophecy." One of the highest ranked search words for Rapture Ready is "www.raptureready.com."

In one sense, it is silly for someone to go to search engines and enter the full domain address of a site they are trying to find. It would be much easier to simply type the address directly into the domain window of Internet Explorer or Netscape. Unfortunately, many people simply don't have the detailed understanding of how to navigate the Internet, so they lack the ability to make use of this time-saving option.

To one person, the situation with the Web address is as simple as figuring out the color of George Washington's white horse. To another, the matter is as foggy as someone trying to guess the atomic weight of the element palladium.

By analogy, there is an equally large gap of understanding in the world of prophecy. Most people have a very limited grasp of prophecy. Even among Christians, most of them have no idea what will happen during the Tribulation or what the number 666 implies.

Sometimes Simpler Is Superior

One of the main reasons why Billy Graham is said to be the most successful evangelist of the twentieth century, preaching to more than 210 million people in more than 185 countries and territories, is that he has simply preached the "Christ crucified" message with a call for repentance. Far too many evangelists try to make the Gospel more appealing by adding their own clever spin on what they're trying to get across. Thereby, they become supercalifragilisticexpealidociousistic with their messages.

To become a Christian, all a person needs to do is realize his sinful state, ask Jesus to be his Savior, and then follow Jesus' examples of pure living. We can explain Christ's saving process even more simply. On all American currency there are the words "In God We Trust." If we were to personalize this statement in everything we do by saying, "In God I Trust"—and really mean it—we would not go wrong.

Supercalifragilisticexpealidociousization

We've noticed three main areas where man has supercalifragilisticexpialidociousized the Christian message: words, rituals, and traditions.

⊕ **Words** Throughout the Church Age, scholarly men have spent a good deal of time putting together an elaborate list of religious words. By adding all these new terms to Christianity, the intellectual thinkers of the Church have slowly transformed the once-simple Gospel message into a complex matter. How can any Christian expect to reach the common man with words like exegesis, hagiography, examologesis, hydroparastatae, soteriology, or anthropomorphism?

Sometimes we use big words to get people's attention. We entitled this chapter "Supercalifragilisticexpialidocious-ism" to do just that. At other times, complex words can be used to inject humor. One well-known prophecy speaker, just for laughs, has a favorite tongue twister he likes to pitch to his audience. He will get up and say, "Well friends, today we're going to think anew about the contemporaneous implications of psychophysical monism."

Unfortunately, humor and attention getting aren't always the goals of Christian speakers who use big words. One situation involved a preacher who wasn't joking with his audience. This minister used $10 words whenever he spoke. For example, instead of saying "prophecy," he would say "eschatology"; instead of using the word "Gospel," he would use "exegesis." And it wasn't "Jesus" he was studying; it was "Christology."

The host of a local cable program frequently had a certain preacher on his show as a guest speaker. The host, whose name was Joe, said that he received a number of complaints from viewers about his guest's choice of vocabulary. After telling the preacher to tone down his high-sounding talk, and not getting any compliance, Joe finally decided not to have him on the show anymore. Joe later learned that some people who attended the minister's church had stopped going because he was using those annoying, graduate-level words.

You might be wondering, "Why was this joker shooting himself in the foot?" The reason the minister was using the big words was, most likely, simple pride. He obviously was a know-it-all. In the end, his smart talk only made him look foolish.

⊕ **Rituals** The dictionary describes Christian rituals as the use of symbols, gestures, objects, words, and music to involve the community in a church function. The original purpose of Christian rituals was to symbolize or represent a certain aspect of the faith. What has happened, in many cases, is that rituals have become a substitute for true Christianity.

One good example of how rituals have replaced God's original intent is the idea that being baptized in water means you're saved. Instead of relying on the blood of Jesus to wash them clean, some folks believe that a dunking in earthly water has the power to make them ready for Heaven. Many people live in a way that totally opposes the Gospel message, yet because they were baptized in water, they believe they have guaranteed their salvation. For instance, one woman wants her baptismal certificate placed in her hand when she dies.

The coauthors of *Are You Rapture Ready?* believe strongly that followers of Christ should participate in water baptism. Terry James was baptized once in a church baptistry. Todd Strandberg has, so far in his life, been baptized on three different occasions. He was baptized in the name of the Father, Son, and Holy Ghost; in the name of Jesus; and while on a tour of the Holy Land, he was baptized in the Jordan River.

None of these baptisms has any power to save their eternal souls. Apparently, if rituals saved, after being baptized so many times, Todd should be able to freely rob banks and still keep his salvation.

Anyone who holds to the sole requirement of water baptism for salvation should ponder the situation involving the thief on the cross. The so-called "good" thief asked Jesus to remember him when Jesus went into His kingdom. He asked Jesus to save his soul, not his body. That thief was saved and never saw a drop of water to drink, much less to be dipped in or sprinkled by.

Rituals cannot save us from our sins; they only act to hide them. You can put a priestly robe on pornography king Larry Flynt, have Charles Manson do the rosary, or have the president of the United States recite the Lord's Prayer in Latin and change nothing. If you fail to reach the heart of a man, any changes you make on his outside are meaningless.

⊕ **Traditions** From the very beginning, men's traditions have threatened the spreading of the Gospel message. In most cases, when some people add a tradition to the Word of God, they have no concrete Scripture to support their action. It is all just made-up supercalifragilisticexpealidociousism.

"It's not valid if it's not in the Bible." This should be every Christian's motto.

The teaching of purgatory is an example. Where did this come from? You can look from Genesis to Revelation and not find any hint that teaches there's a halfway place for those who need to suffer, pray their way to Heaven, or wait for their family members to give enough money that their dearly departed can get out of purgatory.

While searching through a library, we found a book on purgatory and read through it to find out where people got this teaching. The book offered four possible explanations:

1. Tradition—the book said simply that purgatory was "traditionally taught."

2. History—the book cited a reference from one of the "lost books" that said we should "pray for the dead" (2 Maccabees 12:46).

3. Word of mouth—the book said that purgatory exists, in essence, "because the Council of Trent said so."

4. A saintly vision—the book said St. Francis of Rome, through divine revelation, claimed to have gotten a peek at this place—at both its upper and lower levels.

None of these explanations for the existence of a purgatory has anything to do with the Holy Bible. Before the "church fathers" dreamed up the concept of purgatory, they should have read Revelation 22:18: "For I testify unto everyone who hears the words of the prophecy of this book: If anyone adds to these things, God will add to him the plagues that are written in this book."

We've noticed that several traditions of men have been creeping into the Church in recent years. Some of these are environmentalism, liberation theology, politics, psychology, self-esteem, and the false health and wealth prosperity gospel. These are all add-ons that only choke true Christian doctrine.

Paul warns believers to be wary of strange new doctrines: "As we have said before, so now I say again, if anyone preaches any other gospel to you than what you have received, let him be accursed" (Galatians 1:9).

TROUBLING TRICK OF TYRANTS

Keeping their victims in ignorance by suppressing education and by bombarding them with half-lies propaganda has historically been a successful tool in the tyrant's bag of tricks. Nazi propaganda minister Joseph Goebbels put into action the words of psychologist and philosopher William James: "If one shouts a lie long enough and loud enough, people will eventually accept it as true."

Many politicians are in that business of shouting long and loud today. And, true to James's observation, people fall right into line with the media-assisted politically-correct-speak in most instances. Although this is to be expected with politicians, we suppose, it becomes most disturbing when the clergy use the same tricks of the tyrant's trade. The result is even more destructive when the theologians employ such propaganda techniques.

The ultimate political tyrants, like Hitler and Goebbels, used words to destroy their victims' wills and, eventually, their lives. The theologians who deliberately proclaim deceptive teachings and outright lies eventually contribute to the destruction of souls.

Bible Babble

Perhaps the best example of tyranny and the use of words to control people can be found in the history of the printed word. The invention of the Gutenberg printing press is at the heart of that history.

The Uneducated Masses

People were under the oppressively pious thumb of the Catholic clergy, captives of their own ignorance, until in the mid fifteenth century Johannes Gutenberg invented a press that allowed for the mass production of books. Even with its invention, people were kept in the dark on religious matters until the Bible became generally available to them around 1454–1455.

Church leaders had exclusive access to the Bible before the printed word eventually got down to the people. Mass was presided over in Latin. The Scriptures were in Latin. Only the Catholic clergy were able to understand the language. This created a theocratic dictatorship of sorts.

Whatever the dictates of the Church, the people couldn't refute them because they couldn't understand the Latin, which, in any case, was never offered to the masses, except when the clergy translated it to their flocks in carefully scripted sermons. And, be sure, that was done in the finest tradition of supercalifragilisticexpealidociousism.

THE SUPREME SUPERCALIFRAGILISTIC-EXPEALIDOCIOUSISMIST

Bible prophecy tells us that Antichrist will be the most persuasive speechmaker in the history of man. He will, in fact, promise to bring Heaven to Earth. He will claim to be God himself! The bigger his words and promises, the more people will love and follow him.

The Beast That Speaks

Most people of the world will listen to what the Antichrist has to say. As a matter of fact, they will hang on his every word, because he will have a supernatural gift of gab (*Find It Fast:* Daniel 7:8; Revelation 13:5). The supernatural source: Satan.

Antichrist's supercalifragilisticexpealidociousism will speak right to the lustful minds of the Tribulation era. Millions will adore him and ultimately worship him, Bible prophecy says. He will be a speaker for the Toastmasters Club to die for. In fact, millions will die because of him. Bible prophecy says that he will destroy many people (*Find It Fast:* Daniel 8:25). He will mesmerize most of the world's population with his great words. People will follow him like sheep to a slaughter.

RAPTURE READINESS

It is an understatement to say that those who leave Earth in the Rapture will, thankfully, not hear this gentleman's glowing words of false promises. Antichrist will, shortly after coming to power, make Attila the Hun, Adolf Hitler, Joseph Stalin, Mao Tse-tung, Pol Pot, Idi Amin, and all other dictators who have ever lived look like seventh-grade delinquents when compared to him.

"Rapture readiness" never looked better!

BE TAKEN
OR
FORSAKEN!

CHAPTER 6

In the Twinkling

A young mother will be walking the aisles of a Wal-Mart store, or perhaps another large discount store, with her two-year-old daughter riding securely and happily in the shopping cart while they both look over all the brightly packaged goods on the shelves. A businessman will be entering an on-ramp to a freeway near Los Angeles, giving a nervous glance to his left to make sure he will have room to merge smoothly into the flow of traffic.

Half a world away, the captain of a 747, having just received permission to take off, will push the throttles fully forward and the gigantic bird will begin its roll between the runway lights that appear to come together in a sharp point in the distant darkness. A mother-to-be will reach for a ringing telephone, a broad smile on her face anticipating talking with her husband who had promised to call once he was settled in his hotel where his company is holding its quarterly sales meeting. Then, in a split-second, it will happen . . .

A surgeon in a Boston hospital who has just started moving his scalpel along the man's chest suddenly finds the blade cutting only air. The patient is gone!

A mortician in Dallas recoils in astonishment when the suit he is smoothing on the corpse collapses. The body is no longer there!

The mother pushing the cart in the store turns back toward the basket with the items she has gotten from the shelf. Her little girl is missing! Only her toddler's colorful little dress and shoes remain in the cart in a crumpled heap. The woman's scream pierces the air, joining other screams of similar panic reverberating throughout the store.

At the same moment the commuting businessman in Los Angeles sees the big semi rig directly in front of him swerve sharply right and begin tumbling down the steep embankment while the roadways ahead and on either side of him explode with violent wrecks.

Precisely at that instant the copilot in the 747's right seat panics when he realizes that the huge jet, now screaming down the runway at more than 100 miles per hour, is totally out of control, its pilot having disappeared!

The young father-to-be is shouting into the telephone, wanting to know what is wrong with his wife, whom he hears crying hysterically. She has fallen to the floor and is desperately groping her abdomen, nearly insane because she cannot feel the baby who is no longer in her womb.

Billions of people around the world will suffer shocks similar to those depicted above. Or they will awaken to find

they live in a world phenomenally different than the one
they knew when they went to bed the night before.
—William Terry James, General Editor, *Prophecy at Ground Zero*
(Lancaster, PA: Starburst Publishers, 2002)

Marge had referred to the innocents. The doctor assumed it
was the Rapture. Steve had pooh-poohed space aliens. But
how could you rule out anything at this point?

His mind was already whirring with ideas for the story
behind the disappearances. Talk about the assignment of a
lifetime!

—Left Behind

DUMBFOUNDING DISAPPEARANCE

Cameron "Buck" Williams, a journalist for an international news organization, is dumbfounded by the disappearances, like everybody
else. Whatever happened, it came suddenly, and profoundly affected
the entire world. The instant vanishing of millions was probably the
greatest news story of all time!

The fictional account from the novel brings to life the prophecy
and promise made by Jesus Christ: "Therefore you also be ready, for
the Son of Man is coming at an hour you do not expect" (Luke 12:40).

The ascended and fully revealed Lord of lords and King of
kings, speaking to the prophet John from Heaven, promised: "And,
behold, I am coming quickly, and my reward is with me, to give to
every one according to his work" (Revelation 22:12). Christ said
again: "He who testifies to these things says, 'Surely I am coming
quickly'" (Revelation 22:20).

TIMING THE TWINKLING

Paul the apostle put the prophetic stopwatch on the Rapture. He told us just how suddenly Christ will come for His bride, the Church. He wrote to the Christians of Corinth and to those throughout the centuries to our time: "Behold, I tell you a mystery: We shall not all sleep, but we shall all be changed—in a moment, in the twinkling of an eye, at the last trumpet. For the trumpet will sound, and the dead will be raised incorruptible, and we shall be changed" (1 Corinthians 15:51–52).

Most who read Paul's description of the Rapture think it means at the speed it takes to blink the eyelids together and open them again.

Wrong! It's much, much faster than that.

LIFE IN THE FAST, FAST LANE

The Rapture will be the highway to eternal life in the fastest fast lane imaginable. That life will begin with a sudden—and we *do* mean sudden—snatching up of believers into the regions above Earth to meet Christ.

Not only is the Rapture going to be super sudden; it will be—as said before—a total surprise. It's imminent, meaning it will happen without any prophetic sign to announce that it's coming.

HOW FAST IS FAST?

The following description makes the analogy between the "twinkling of an eye" and the basic building block particle of all things in the universe.

"How fast is [the 'twinkling of an eye']? Well the dictionary shows us that the 'twinkling' of an eye is 1/100th of a second, the batting of an eyelash. But careful study of the scriptures shows us otherwise. Let's take a look.

"The original Greek word for moment is 823 atomos (at'-om-os); from 1 (as a negative particle) and the base of 5114; uncut, i.e. (by implication) indivisible [an 'atom' of time]: KJV—moment.

"It is the word from which we derive our modern English word of 'atom.' It literally means: uncut, indivisible, an 'atom' of time. In other words, this time frame, or 'atom' of time, cannot be measured by human means. It cannot be divided or cut. It will happen so fast, that there is no measure of time for it."

("Speed of Rapture," raptureme.com Web site: http://www.raptureme.com/resource/speed.html.)

The analogy is a bit complex for most of us who had trouble with elementary science and general math, but you get the picture. The Rapture is going to be quite sudden.

IMMINENCE

In doing some research on the doctrine of imminence, we noticed that few people take the time to actually define what prophetic imminence means. First let's look at the general definition of the key word "imminent": "The quality or condition of being about to occur."

Imminence, as it relates to Bible prophecy, simply means that the return of Jesus Christ for the Church can happen at any moment. There are no warning signs or indications of a short-term countdown. Christians should, according to the Bible, remain on alert for Christ's coming for them twenty-four hours a day, seven days a week.

If a husband tells his wife he is coming to pick her up after he gets off work at 4 P.M., and that she should be ready to meet him, his coming is at hand. That is, he could return at any moment after 4 P.M. His wife may not know the exact moment he will be coming for her, but she knows that every minute after 4 P.M. his arrival becomes more imminent.

NO WIFELY WARNINGS

If the husband had told his wife that before he arrived at her location, he would call her on his cell phone or send someone ahead to announce his coming, she would have no real reason to be actively looking for him. Her focus would instead be on waiting for one of those two precursors to transpire.

THE WIFE TO WATCH

FIND IT FAST

Jesus, just before His death, burial, resurrection, and ascension, told the Church: "Therefore you also be ready, for the Son of Man is coming at an hour you do not expect" (Matthew 24:44). He said nothing about watching for a peace treaty, the Antichrist, the false prophet, the four horsemen of the Apocalypse, the seven scrolls, the seven trumpets, or the seven bowls judgments to first play out during the Tribulation. Jesus told the Church simply to watch for His return (*Find It Fast:* Mark 13:37).

THE GRANDDADDY OF PROOFS

The Pre-Tribulation Rapture is the only view that allows for the Rapture to be imminent in its timing. All the other views of the Rapture require a number of prophetic occurrences to take place before the Rapture can be considered imminent. Any conditions for the Rapture, it should be obvious to anyone, completely destroy the imminence of the event. Nowhere in the Bible does Jesus tell His Church to watch for the events of the Tribulation. He tells His own to watch for Him!

CHRIST AND CHURCH

Bible prophecy does, of course, warn of the events of the Apocalypse in many places, particularly in the book of Revelation. But when those judgments begin taking place, as outlined in Revelation, the Church—all believers of the Church Age—is no longer in view.

Jesus Christ, in the first three chapters of the book of Revelation, talks directly to His Church. John the apostle hears the words "Come up here!" in Revelation 4:1, and the Church is not mentioned again until chapter 19, *after* the Tribulation and all God's judgments have run their course.

Again, the Church is mentioned by name nineteen times in chapters 1 through 3. It isn't mentioned again until chapter 19, which describes Christians returning from Heaven with Christ to set up His millennial kingdom. The Church isn't mentioned in all that vast interim expanse of Revelation because the Church is in Heaven, not on Earth, during that horrible period of time. To be looking for the imminent return of Christ, you have to believe in a Pre-Trib Rapture.

Jesus repeatedly said that His return for the Church would be a surprise. The Lord even went beyond surprise by saying that He would return "as a thief" and at a time when believers generally won't be expecting Him to come for them.

"But of that day and hour no one knows, not even the angels of heaven, but My Father only" (Matthew 24:36).

RAPTURE RIDICULERS

Most of those who teach that there is no sudden, surprise coming of Christ, ridicule such a concept by sarcastically referring to it as a "secret Rapture." They hang on with teeth, fingernails, and toenails to the Scripture: "For as the lightning comes from the east and flashes to the west, so also will the coming of the Son of Man be" (Matthew 24:27).

Here's another favorite verse used by detractors of the belief in an imminent return of Christ: "Behold, He is coming with clouds, and every eye will see Him, even they who pierced Him. And all the tribes of the earth will mourn because of Him" (Revelation 1:7).

On the other hand, they avoid the vast number of Bible verses describing a sudden, any-minute return of Christ for His Church. They fail to understand the two distinct phases of His coming again. The first phase: the Rapture of His Church; the second phase: His coming at the end of the Tribulation.

The two phases can't be one and the same. Each phase has distinctive purposes and activities.

THE THIEF ANALOGY

Rapture doctrine despisers mockingly reject the proposition that Christ's coming again will happen in any way other than how they perceive it. They most often proclaim that it is supreme foolishness to try to tell the world that God will deal with this planet in any kind of a disruptive way. After all, other than what the Bible says about His past interventions, everything has gone along as it always has.

THE RAPTURE	THE SECOND COMING
Christ comes in the air.	His foot touches down on Earth.
His Church goes up to meet Him in the air.	His Church returns with Him to Earth.
He comes at a time no one but God the Father knows.	The exact day of His return is known, during the Tribulation.
No one left behind on Earth will see Him.	Everyone will see Him.
Christ is described as the Bridegroom.	He is described as the King of kings, and Lord of lords.
Rapture will be a time of joy.	Second Coming will be a violent conclusion to man's ultimate war.
Rapture will be a time of the "marriage supper of the Lamb."	Second Coming will be a time when the scavengers dine on the flesh of rebellious people.
Christ gives rewards to Christians.	Christ punishes the rebels with righteous judgment.

There have been, of course, the scientists tell us, some cataclysmic meteorite strikes that might have destroyed dinosaurs, etc., but who among us have seen even those happenstances of chance? Bible prophecies of God's future interference into the affairs of mankind must, they say, be considered in spiritual or allegorical terms, not as literal.

PETER POINTS A FINGER

The Apostle Peter had something to say about our time. He points a prophetic finger directly at that type of mocking of God's prophetic Word. "Knowing this first: that scoffers will come in the last days, walking according to their own lusts, and saying, 'Where is the promise of His coming? For since the fathers fell asleep, all things continue as they were from the beginning of creation'" (2 Peter 3:3–4).

The Rapture detractors cling only to Scriptures they believe put forward their position. But they are in error. They explain away any reference to a sudden, surprise coming of Christ as being simply symbolic. The use of the term "thief in the night" and "as a thief," when describing Christ's coming again, somehow passes between their ears like coffee through a cup with no bottom.

TWIST ON THE TWINKLING

The Rapture will be an event of exhilaration for Christians. Paul the apostle prophesies that fact, as we have seen. There is the other side of the Rapture, however. Jesus himself minces no words on the matter. He tells of a sudden, startling, and imminent return: "Remember therefore how you have received and heard; hold fast and repent. Therefore if you will not watch, I will come upon you as a thief, and you will not know what hour I will come upon you" (Revelation 3:3).

He issues a stern warning to Christians who are living lives that are not in accordance with God's ways. The "twinkling" will seemingly be a little like being touched by an exposed 220-volt wire to those of God's children who are not living right, and who are not looking for Christ to come for them.

In this instance, Jesus likens His coming to a thief breaking in unannounced. Nobody likes a thief paying Him a surprise visit! Obviously, the Rapture will be less than exhilaration for those who are not ready.

The Lord says further: "Behold, I am coming as a thief. Blessed is he who watches, and keeps his garments, lest he walk naked and they see his shame" (Revelation 16:15). Now, Jesus speaks to those who are "Rapture ready." He commends them and blesses them for watching for His sudden, imminent coming.

PAUL PULLS NO PUNCHES

Paul puts his own twist on the Rapture promise. He, like Jesus, uses the "thief" terminology when he says: "For you yourselves know perfectly that the day of the Lord so comes as a thief in the night" (1 Thessalonians 5:2).

He says here that Christians have no excuse to not be "Rapture ready." Christians are told plainly in God's Word that Christ is coming "as a thief." That is, He will be unannounced, and it will not be altogether pleasant for those who aren't ready. Christians know this perfectly well, Paul says. They should know it perfectly well through reading and studying the Bible. God has put it there for them to know.

PETER'S TWIST ON THE TWINKLING

The big fisherman, Peter, put the "in the twinkling of an eye" Rapture in its proper place, so far as God's prophetic timeline is concerned. He said, "But the day of the Lord will come as a thief in the night, in which the heavens will pass away with a great noise, and the elements will melt with fervent heat; both the earth and the works that are in it will be burned up" (2 Peter 3:10).

Jesus and Paul said Christ will come as a thief. That is, He will be totally unexpected by the world as a whole, and even by many Christians who are walking with the world, and not with God. These Christians will have somewhat of a problem when coming face to face with their Savior and Lord. Peter prophesies that the end of all things that involve present-day Planet Earth will begin with the "in the twinkling" event known as Rapture.

The end of the world as we know it will begin, he says, with the "thief in the night" coming of Christ. That's the Pre-Tribulation Rapture!

The wrap-up of God's concluding chapter of the greatest story ever told will run its course. Finally, God will purge the Earth with fire in preparation for making it a totally new creation. The "thief in the night" event could happen at any moment, in the twinkling of an eye. Again, Jesus said: "Therefore you also be ready, for the Son of Man is coming at an hour you do not expect" (Matthew 24:44).

IF YOU'RE
STILL HERE
IT'S TIME
TO FEAR!

CHAPTER 7

The Greatest
Media Event of All Time

Buck leaped to his feet, Steve right with him, along with dozens of other members of the press.

Something had happened in the disappearances of loved ones all over the globe. Journalism might never be the same. Oh, there would be skeptics and those who worshiped objectivity. But what had happened to brotherly love? What had become of depending on one another? What had happened to the brotherhood of men and nations?

It was back. And while no one expected that the press might become the public-relations agency for a new political star, Carpathia certainly had them in his corner this afternoon . . .

Young Nicolae was at an emotional, fevered pitch.

. . . Carpathia had brought the entire crowd to its feet in full voice and applause, press and representative alike. Even the cynical Steve Plank and Buck Williams continued to clap and cheer, never once appearing embarrassed at their loss of detached objectivity.

—Left Behind

LEADER CAPTIVATES THE WORLD

World media are portrayed as joining wholeheartedly in Nicolae Carpathia's (the Antichrist's) call for world unity. The Rapture has taken millions of people, and order must be made of the chaos that resulted.

Buck Williams and his colleague, Steve Plank, find themselves caught up in the great leader's hypnotic words about the brother-hood of mankind. Their journalistic integrity goes out the window, along with the lately departed who were taken in the Rapture. Barri-ers separating news reporters from newsmakers are suddenly broken down by the handsome, dynamic young man calling for unification and universal love.

Talk About a Great Story!

It is easy to speculate about how such a story as the disappearance of a sizable chunk of the world's population could throw the news es-tablishment into hyperdrive. Think for a moment about any story that catches their attention. Remember how the media report, from every imaginable perspective, things like the Bush-Gore Florida "hanging chad"/"dimpled chad" presidential election ballot fray? The frantic coverage of the attacks on the World Trade Center towers and the Pentagon serve as an even better example of how obsessive the media are, by their very nature. The Rapture will give fodder for unprecedented coverage.

Supreme Intervention

It is impossible to anticipate the total effects of the Rapture. However, Hal Lindsey, author of *The Late, Great Planet Earth* and well-known prophecy scholar, said:

"I believe the next intervention of God into human history will be that time when Jesus says, 'Come up here!' And only believers will understand what the noise meant. The world will hear some noise, but they won't understand it. Then suddenly, all over the world, people will disappear . . . I believe God is going to do it just like that in order to shake them up and let them know that something dramatic has happened. If God is going to remove His ambassadors, you can expect there will be some repercussions that will shake people up and I really believe that when every living believer is snatched out, there's going to be planes crashing, cars crashing; there's going to be all kinds of weird things happening because God wants to shake up the world and let them know that something supernatural has intervened" (Hal Lindsey, *The Rapture Factor*, audio/video, Hal Lindsey Ministries).

Pundits' Paradise

To repeat: What a news story! Journalists will be calling pundits from every walk of life to try and explain this one. It will indeed be the greatest media event of all time. While brotherhood and unity, and all that, will doubtless be the eventual message of the world's leadership, the earliest stages of recovery from the Rapture will likely produce great chaos.

News Bulletin

Network anchors will appear on TV screens almost as suddenly as the people around the world disappeared. While video, both live and taped, quickly cuts from one frantic scene to another, the smooth delivery of the anchors will continue, their voices perhaps raised an octave or two above their usually flat, reportorial tones.

Out-Hollywooding Hollywood

Astonishing stories will unfold from that point. Personal witnesses to the vanishing and many videotaped recordings will show the surreal truth of the phenomenon. Life on Earth will forever have changed in ways that will be dissected in excruciating detail over the following minutes, hours, and days.

Nothing Hollywood could cook up could ever match the magnitude of the event. Speculation will go from the absurd to the sublime. Some might proclaim the extraterrestrials have finally abducted massive numbers instead of fooling around with only an abduction here and there. Evolutionary scientists might speculate that it is some sort of quantum leap. Futurists will propose a quantum leap of another kind, that of leaping from mortality to a "higher mind-consciousness," as has been promised by the ascended masters for many years.

Dinosaur Ditto?

Yet others will ponder whether it was another cosmic interference, like the comet or meteorite believed to have destroyed the dinosaurs. Ministers will, most likely, be asked to analyze whether this could possibly be the long-debated Rapture. These—being open-minded, critical thinkers—will likely say that the Rapture is a possibility, but that that scenario is highly unlikely. They will most likely come down on the side of the scientists and New Age postulations. Probably, the ministers will opt for a combination of a number of theories, so as not to offend anyone involved in the speculation.

Compromising Clergy

Left-behind ministers will possibly propose two theological answers, figuring, of course, both the opinions of the scientific community and futurist thought into their suggestions. They might say that God took those who had earned sainthood through good works here on Earth. Or they might say that God, or the "great universal mind," took the disruptive forces from the planet so that mankind could get on with the business of building a peaceful Earth. Probably the latter will win out in the thinking of most of Earth's clergy.

Peace Finally Gets a Chance

Weird yet exciting things will undoubtedly progress from that point. According to the Bible and its prophecies, people will believe this

The prophet Daniel foretells the rise of the "king of fierce countenance," the Antichrist. He will stand out in a field of great world leaders, like a professional basketball center would stand out in a kindergarten class. His personality, personal charisma, and good looks will charm all of those in the media, and almost everyone else.

As already mentioned, he will be an orator with unparalleled speaking abilities. He will know exactly how to delude with words, and he will "understand dark sentences," as the Bible puts it. Satan will be his guiding force in every aspect of his power.

The great world politician will guarantee to produce world peace, a promise onto which the world will latch. But, ultimately, through that peace—which will be a phony peace—he will destroy many people. Chief among those people destroyed will be the Jews, whom he will seek to completely eradicate.

will be a time to "give peace a chance" at last, as the late John Lennon once pleaded. Nicolae Carpathia—or whatever the name of the great world leader that emerges from all the confusion—will promise peace, prosperity, and a world that will evolve to Heaven on Earth.

Peace Decomposes

However, the Scriptures say that end-time things, the great world leader, and the process of peace will develop much differently.

Everyone left behind after the disappearance, not just the Jewish people, should worry about this guy and his regime. Bible prophecy says, "For when they say, 'Peace and safety!' then sudden destruction comes upon them, as labor pains upon a pregnant woman. And they shall not escape" (1 Thessalonians 5:3).

People who look to the world leader and his regime, and not to Jesus Christ, for their well-being won't find peace; they'll run into unprecedented troubles. Not only will Antichrist be acting in tyrannical ways while he conquers the world, but God himself will be sending judgments upon the planet. Those judgments will come like painful contractions of a woman in labor, Bible prophecy says.

SATAN SUMMONS SUPERMAN

You've heard of the knight on the white horse coming to rescue the damsel in distress. That scene has a modern twist which puts it as a "rider on a white horse" coming to rescue us all. The Bible uses a rider on a white horse to symbolize the Antichrist coming onto the scene at the beginning of the Tribulation: "And I looked, and behold, a white horse. He who sat on it had a bow; and a crown was given to him, and he went out conquering, and to conquer" (Revelation 6:2).

The self-assured global leader rides majestically onto the world stage. He doesn't look to be the beast, as he is later described. He will have every appearance of being able to deliver on his great words of promise.

The Rapture will have set the stage for this superman to take the spotlight. Let's take a deeper look into the circumstances under which the world leader will come to power.

POST-RAPTURE PICTURE

Many who study the world situation today see the stage for post-Rapture Earth already far along in preparation for the coming new world order. Those dramatic preparations are, themselves, often spectacular media events.

⊕ **Russia Rumbles Again** One such example is the sudden disintegration of the former Soviet Union. Prophecy watchers saw the collapse and the reconstitution under its historical name, Russia, as significant. Ezekiel, chapters 38 and 39, emerged to the forefront of our time, many prophecy scholars believe.

Briefly, Ezekiel the prophet spoke of an invasion led by a person named Gog, the leader of a place called "Rosh," into the Middle East and Israel. "Rosh" is an ancient term from which the word "Russia" comes. With the formation of the Islamic states along Russia's southern borders, it now becomes clear that Russia, with its CIS (Commonwealth of Independent States) coalition, could decide to attack the Middle East and Israel in order to gain oil and other riches, just as prophesied in Ezekiel 38 and 39.

⊕ **Israel Reborn** Israel, of course, had to be back in the geopolitical picture as a nation before this could be possible. That happened on May 14, 1948, with that nation's rebirth in its biblical homeland.

⊕ **Rome Revives** The reviving of the spirit of the ancient Roman Empire, through the developing European Union, is another signal that the stage is being set for a post-Rapture new world order.

The bottom line is this: Planet Earth, with the many prophetic signals already presented in this book, is in position to welcome a regime that will offer to create order from the chaos that will surely follow the sudden disappearance of millions around the globe.

WARNING TO WATCH

Only God knows the year, month, and date of the Rapture. Jesus himself stated plainly that knowledge of this event is the Father's alone. Therefore, it is not our place to speculate on His perfect timing. Because the Earth is a spherical body with twenty-four time zones, however, we can say with 100 percent certainty the Rapture will take place at every hour of the day. It will occur in the morning, at noon, in the evening, and in the dead of the night.

Jesus seemed to have just a little bit of sport with His coming suddenly, when teaching on the subject. He said in Mark 13:35: "Watch therefore, for you do not know when the master of the house is coming—in the evening, at midnight, at the crowing of the rooster, or in the morning . . ."

Someday, all born-again believers are going to suddenly find themselves caught up into the heavenly realm to meet the Lord. The only preparation for this shocking event, according to the Lord Jesus Christ, is to be constantly vigilant.

Here are some thoughts on things that will likely occur when God calls the Church home.

⊕ **Things Left Behind** You've heard the saying "You can't take it with you" about your valuables and death. This will be true of the Rapture as well. There has been much speculation over whether or not clothing and various other personal items, like hearing aids and pacemakers, will be left behind. After the Rapture, the material possessions of those who have disappeared will, no doubt, be a matter of amazement.

The novel *Left Behind* depicts piles of clothing lying on passenger seats and floors of the 747. Clothing, shoes, and all sorts of prosthetic devices, including glasses, etc., are found on the ground, wherever people disappeared.

Does the Bible indicate that such things will happen when the Rapture occurs? Is there indication that material things will be left behind?

Remember that Paul the apostle wrote: "For this corruptible must put on incorruption, and this mortal must put on immortality" (1 Corinthians 15:53).

FIND IT FAST

He prophesies that things of this world, be they human bodies or anything else, must take on a changed form if they are to go into Heaven. As a matter of fact, we know from watching space walkers in their bulky, protective suits, that things must be changed a bit for man to even go into space.

Clothes are imperfect, and cannot inherit the kingdom of Heaven. They are destined to be left behind, because they could not survive going into that other dimension.

When the Rapture happens, it follows that all material things of Earth will stay behind. Clothing and all the other things that adorn or prop up the human body will fall

ELIJAH'S EXAMPLE

The story of Elijah, to many Bible students, foreshadows the Rapture. The Bible said that God took Elijah to Heaven while the old prophet was still alive. He was "translated," which means "changed" or "raptured":

"[Elisha] also took up the mantle of Elijah that had fallen from him, and went back and stood by the bank of the Jordan. Then he took the mantle of Elijah that had fallen from him, and struck the water, and said, 'Where is the Lord God of Elijah'? . . ." (2 Kings 2:13).

Elijah's mantle (his cloak, which had significance in his role as prophet) fell to the ground when he was suddenly taken from the presence of his protégé, Elisha. Obviously, Elijah couldn't take it with him.

where the person was but is not, as was said about Enoch in Genesis, chapter 5.

⊕ **Great Numbers Gone** Only God knows how many people are actually ready for the Rapture. The Word of God uses the word "few" in describing the number of people who will find salvation, so it is likely that the same "few" will apply to the people turning up missing.

Because Europe and Asia have a low number of confessing, born-again believers, the Rapture rate will likely be much lower in these two areas. Many central African nations will probably see a higher percentage of their citizens get raptured. Nations like Zambia have a very large Christian population.

One thing for sure, the sudden vanishing of great numbers of people while they go about their human activities will profoundly affect many parts of the world.

⊕ **Wide-Eyed Eyewitnesses** The Rapture will obviously come as an immense surprise to everyone remaining behind on Earth. The first indication that the Rapture has taken place will be people witnessing the disappearance of believers.

⊕ **Transportation Turmoil** One of the most attention-getting consequences of the Rapture will be the huge number of automobile accidents that will result. Removal of millions of drivers will, without question, create chaos on the roads. Just imagine, for example, the Rapture occurring during rush hour on Chicago or Houston's loops. How about at rush hour on the New Jersey or Pennsylvania turnpikes?

A popular bumper sticker reads, IN CASE OF RAPTURE, THIS CAR WILL BE UNMANNED. Funny, but profound.

⊕ **Remarkably Memorable News Story** Whenever a disaster takes place, most people turn to radio, television, and Internet news outlets for the latest information. Some of the most shocking news stories of modern times—for that matter, of all time—have been President John F. Kennedy's assassination, the attempted assassination of President Reagan, the NASA *Challenger* explosion, and the 9/11 terrorist attacks. Millions of people were glued to live news reports as news surrounding the tragedies unfolded.

The Rapture will be a challenge for the intellectual/rationale-dominated press to cover. Over the years, both authors of this book have been interviewed by many media folks. It's always interesting to note how little knowledge many of these people demonstrate about Bible prophecy. Their interest is usually only stimulated when something dramatic happens that might result in an Armageddon-type conflict. So it's easy to understand their ignorance of the vast body of prophetic truth.

Journalism schools and on-the-job-training force their minds—individually and collectively—into what they consider to be a realistic worldview. Religion and prophecy are not rationale-based, therefore they don't warrant the same degree of consideration as more weighty matters. At least, that seems to be the mainstream news mind-set. They will have an extremely limited understanding of how this supernatural event relates to the Endtime.

⊕ **Rude Awakening** It will probably only take the media a few minutes to become fully aware that something very strange has happened. All news organizations closely monitor emergency radio channels. The reports will quickly mushroom into a confusing chorus of distress calls. The press will instantly have a news event that will be a local, national, and international crisis.

Realization that something has happened that defies logic will, for a time, awaken newspeople to possibilities they had always rejected. Certainly, like the fictional news journalist characters Buck Williams and Steve Plank, reporters around the world will have trouble keeping their objectivity.

⊕ **Puzzled People?** A lot of prophecy writers seem to think the Rapture will be a big mystery to everyone left behind. They speculate that people will think alien abduction is to blame for the disappearances. One poll conducted by *Time* magazine and CNN found that 59 percent of the American population believes the prophecies of Revelation will come true. A third of the people in that same survey said they are closely watching prophecy.

Much information, after all, has been disseminated about these prophetic matters in recent years. For example, many millions of the *Left Behind* series have gotten into the hands of great numbers of people around the world. God would not let a generation face such a time of judgment without adequate warning. He would go against His very character if He failed to give a heads-up to the approaching Apocalypse. God has provided such alerts before every judgment that has ever fallen, for example, His warning to Sodom and Gomorrah, and to the city of Nineveh.

⊕ **People in Panic** After the Rapture takes place, it won't take very long for a large part of the population to realize they've been left behind. Many will probably become hysterical with fear. Others will think the world is going to end shortly. In reality, the Earth won't see any major judgments until the midpoint of the Tribulation.

⊕ **Spiritual Awakening** A spiritual awakening will probably sweep over the land as people find themselves forced to appraise their spiritual condition. Spiritual revival, in this case, means those who remain will turn to Christ for salvation of their souls. It might seem strange to think that a huge conversion to Christianity could break out just ahead of what is predicted to be Earth's greatest period of deception. Such a revival will likely be broad, but very shallow.

This is because the horrors that many people believed would instantly fall upon them won't do so right away. When God doesn't immediately begin to punish the people of Earth, they will likely fall for the deceptive lies of those offering explanations such as "the disappearance had nothing to do with God, or prophecy." The deceivers will undoubtedly be able to turn many people's minds toward believing that the

POST-RAPTURE PROBLEMS

Because the U.S. and Canada have, perhaps, the highest percentage of born-again believers of any industrialized nations, the North American economy will likely suffer a huge body blow when millions vanish. During the darkest days of the Great Depression, the gross domestic product of the U.S. only experienced a 10 percent decline.

After the Rapture, several negative economic factors will almost certainly come into play. The following are some studied speculations on a post-Rapture economy.

⊕ The Rapture alone might automatically imply a 10 percent plunge in economic activity.

⊕ The loss of the "salt of the earth" (a Bible term defining Christians' beneficial qualities) will likely paralyze a number of businesses.

⊕ Nonproductive people who have always been a drag on the economy will, following the Rapture, make up a larger percentage of the general population.

⊕ The psychological shock of the disappearances will severely disrupt the spending habits of folks who find themselves left behind.

⊕ The insurance industry will almost certainly be wiped out.

⊕ Banks and other businesses big and small will have difficulty resolving outstanding debts.

⊕ There will be a sudden overabundance of houses and cars, causing prices for these two key commodities to decline.

⊕ A Rapture-triggered economic implosion could be one primary reason why Uncle Sam is not mentioned as a key player in prophecy. The Rapture could be instrumental in the European Union stepping in to fill the void.

⊕ There will be some sort of dramatic unification of global economic system matters. Monetary rearrangement will likely be a major part of Antichrist's masterstroke for fixing things during that time of crisis.

⊕ Emergency actions by governments will be implemented to restore order. No doubt martial law will be invoked for a time.

⊕ Proposed new, strict laws for governing the masses will, no doubt, run swiftly through the legislative processes of democratic nations.

⊕ Cooperative police and military forces will likely form new, people-controlling alliances on a global scale.

⊕ Satellite, computer, video, and other technologies will quickly develop in the name of restoring order through improved surveillance efforts.

⊕ Many people will likely choose to become Christians as a response to the Rapture. The availability of material on the subject of the Endtime will probably be an important factor in helping people make decisions for Christ. All prophecy books will instantly disappear from bookstores. The demand for prophecy books will be in the tens of millions, but the supply will only be in the thousands. The Internet will be a huge benefit to people seeking information.*

⊕ The Bible, in 2 Thessalonians, chapter 2, tells us that strong delusion will eventually follow the Rapture. One of the leading sources of deception could be the so-called Christian leaders that are left behind. They will be doing their very best to contradict biblical truth. It's pointless to go too far in trying to guess what they will say to rationalize the Rapture, but they will surely have a number of explanations that will all seem logical and soothing to people's troubled minds.

*Because there will surely be an avalanche of data requests following the Rapture, RaptureReady.com, Todd Strandberg's site, is maintained on several servers. The main site, RaptureReady.com, could be rendered lifeless in a few hours or days, but by then, the key articles on crucial prophecy topics will, hopefully, be reproduced on a number of mirror sites. There is a list of mirror sites at the back of this book. Everyone reading this passage after the Rapture automatically has our authorization to reproduce the site's content.

vanishing of friends, family, and acquaintances was all for the best. The wise will at this time be open to anyone that can explain what is actually going on.

It is okay to speculate about events that will follow the Rapture. What will not be good is to experience those dark days firsthand. The Bible tells us that few people will be wise enough to escape the Tribulation hour. Most people will someday learn, all too late, that salvation should have been their highest priority.

The best advice one can give or take is to repent now and avoid the panic and heartache later. The Rapture will indeed be the greatest media event ever. You should want to be a part of the event itself, not the hoopla of the media coverage that will follow.

END-TIME AILMENTS AND RAPTURE-READY RX

Newsaholic Compulsive consumer of prophecy-related news. This person is constantly scanning the news sources, looking for events that relate to the Endtime.

Symptoms Has CNN or Fox News on constantly. Becomes agitated if he or she misses a news update. Breaking news will cause him or her to neglect all social responsibilities.

Treatment One who is news-dependent should become involved in using the information learned to warn people about the Endtime. If world events are trending toward the conclusion of the Church Age, a person who closely follows the news should be motivated to tell the lost people around about Christ.

WHEN CHRIST
RAPTURES,
WHAT'S LEFT
IS YOURS!

CHAPTER 8

You Can Have
the House and the Car

He turned CNN on low so it wouldn't interrupt his sleep, and he watched the world roundup before dozing off. Images from around the globe were almost more than he could take, but news was his business. He remembered the many earthquakes and wars of the last decade and the nightly coverage that was so moving. Now here was a thousand times more of the same, all on the same day. Never in history had more people been killed in one day than those who disappeared all at once. Had they been killed? Were they dead? Would they be back?

Buck couldn't take his eyes, heavy as they were, off the screen as image after image showed disappearances caught on home videotape. From some countries came professional tapes of live television shows in progress, a host's microphone landing atop his empty clothes, bouncing off his shoes, and making a racket as it rolled across the floor. The audience screamed. One of the cameras panned the crowd, which had been at capacity a moment before. Now several seats were empty, clothes draped across them.

Nothing could've been scripted like this, Buck thought, blinking slowly. If somebody tried to sell a screenplay about millions of people disappearing, leaving everything but their bodies behind, it would be laughed off.

—*Left Behind*

A FEW DOLLARS AND *SOME* CHANGE!

Those who firmly believe that God's Word teaches Christ will come for them in the Rapture occasionally hear one version or the other of the good-natured taunt: "When you leave, can I have your car and your house?"

Somebody once reported that when J. P. Morgan, the famous, extremely wealthy financier, died, a newspaper reporter was said to have asked one of Morgan's associates how much money Morgan left. The reply: "He left it all."

We haven't any idea about Mr. Morgan's theological outlook, but his coworker was, pardon the pun, right on the money with his remark. Morgan did, indeed, leave it all. Everyone always leaves it all.

Whether through death, or through that supernatural space shot known as the Rapture, we will leave every bit of money and other material possessions behind in that moment when we face our maker. Raptured Christians will also leave behind a world in chaos. When all of the people who believe in following God's prescription for living are gone, tremendous upheaval will follow.

No matter how much money we make in this life, it is just a few dollars when compared to the stupendous change those have coming who have accepted Jesus Christ as their Savior. That's why the Apostle Paul could say about both Christ and about leaving this life: "Who died for us, that, whether we [live] or [die], we should live together with him. Wherefore comfort yourselves together, and edify one another, just as you also are doing" (1 Thessalonians 5:10–11).

Paul says further: "For I am hard-pressed between the two, having a desire to depart and be with Christ, which is far better. Nevertheless to remain in the flesh is more needful for you" (Philippians 1:23–24).

A *STAR TREK* MOMENT

As we have looked at before several times, Paul said, in describing the moment of Rapture: "Behold, I tell you a mystery: We shall not all sleep, but we shall all be changed—in a moment, in the twinkling of an eye, at the last trumpet. For the trumpet will sound, and the dead will be raised incorruptible, and we shall be changed" (1 Corinthians 15:51–52).

Remember the "Beam me up, Scotty" command of Captain Kirk and Mr. Spock? The transporter beam would lock on the person, who would dissolve to a million sparkling points of electrons or something, and then be reassembled somewhere else.

However the Rapture elevator/transporter works, it will change the Christian so quickly that there will be no sparkling points of light visible to the human eye or camera. The change will take place far faster than Mr. Scott's *Enterprise* transporter system operates. And there will be nothing fictional about the fact that millions will have disappeared.

WORLDWIDE WHIRLWIND

While it will happen so quickly that no one will be able to see the vanishing, many Bible prophecy scholars believe that a noise might accompany the Rapture. That theory is based on scriptural fact, as recorded in the book of Acts.

"When the day of Pentecost had fully come, they were all with one accord in one place. And suddenly there came a sound from heaven, as of a rushing mighty wind, and it filled the whole house where they were sitting. Then there appeared unto them divided tongues, as of fire, and one sat upon each of them. And they were all filled with the Holy Spirit and began to speak with other tongues, as the Spirit gave them utterance" (Acts 2:1–4).

Just as there was the sound of a strong wind when God the Holy Spirit came into believers at Pentecost, as described above, so, many believe, there will be a similar sound when the Holy Spirit leaves with all who are raptured.

The Holy Spirit is omnipresent; that is, He is everywhere, all the time. So, while the Holy Spirit leaves with the believers, He will at the same time remain on Earth. But His function here will be different then than it is now. He will, at Rapture, again function as an outside influence on human history, as He did before Jesus' death on the cross, His burial, resurrection, and ascension to the throne room of God, the Father. The question: Why is all this important?

The key to why it is so important to consider the seemingly tedious details of truth about the Holy Spirit and His change of functions after the Rapture are found in the following verses. Again, the Apostle Paul is the one giving the prophecy.

2 THESSALONIANS 3–10

Paul said that the last days of the Tribulation time won't happen before there is a great departure from belief in Bible truth, and Antichrist is revealed as the man of sin, who is against God, yet claims to be God. He will, in fact, sit in God's temple, to convince people he is God. Paul says that we know what is presently keeping back Antichrist and his total influence. Antichrist will be exposed for who he is at the prophesied time.

The seemingly unexplainable evil of the Antichrist spirit is at work in the world. This will continue until the Holy Spirit, who is the restrainer, moves out of the way when Christ's Church, whom He indwells, is raptured. Then Antichrist will be seen for who he is. Jesus will, at the prophesied time, overcome Antichrist with His great power at His Second Coming. Satan is the one behind the Antichrist's coming upon the world scene, and the lying he will do, and miracles he will perform. Those who refused to believe the truth about Jesus Christ will believe the lie that Antichrist is Savior, and will be judged worthy of hell along with Antichrist, whom they will have worshipped as God.

GOD AS PLANETARY SHERIFF

The Holy Spirit's current job is, in part, to restrain evil in the world. Right now, you might say He has available God's holy handcuffs for use when necessary. It might seem to most of us that He might not have been doing as good a job as He could be doing. However, we must consider God's permissive will. He didn't create robots. He created people to have free will. That is, we are free to love and obey His ways, or not.

As a result of God's patience with the human race, there indeed exist a considerable number of outlaws in this world. That doesn't mean God is at fault; man has only himself to blame for his rebellious nature.

God doesn't force evil people to follow Him, but He does use great restraint against evil to keep it from completely overrunning the Earth. The Bible says that it is the Church—Christ's born-again believers—through whom the restrainer, the Holy Spirit, works. That is keeping the world from going into complete rebellion and debauchery.

When the Church goes to be with Christ at the Rapture, that restraining influence will be gone. God will allow mankind free rein and ultimately the Antichrist will rule over the world that the unrestrained evil will have created.

VIDEO VANISHING

Millions of people will disappear in a millisecond of time. The Rapture will happen so quickly that by the time people begin a downward blink of their eyelids, others will be gone. They will have vanished by the time the eyelids of those left behind start to open again. As we have seen, this is what the Apostle Paul calls "in the twinkling of an eye."

However, just as depicted in the LaHaye/Jenkins novels, television viewers will be able to see disappearances time and time again on videotape. Networks will run the vanishings over and over. It is unlikely that any camera will be capable of slowing action enough to capture anything but a sudden disappearance. Even stop-frame techniques won't show the people dissolve to nothingness. The disappearances will be supernatural, not sleight-of-hand illusions by earthly magicians, or camera special-effects wizardry. No doubt the footage will, like that of the airplanes slamming into the Trade Towers in 2001, dredge up the wrenching emotions of the event every time it is shown.

INSTANT INTERVENTION

This will be God's direct intervention into the affairs of man in a way not seen since the birth of Christ two thousand years ago. This intervention, of course, will be much more spectacular because of the impact the disappearances will instantly have upon our population.

Much will happen in a short time frame on Earth, and in the dimension where time holds no sway. Things will be popping and sizzling at a frantic pace on Planet Earth, while world leaders try to grasp and resolve the many crises that have resulted.

GONE BUT NOT FORGOTTEN

There won't likely be any lives untouched by the Rapture. America will most likely suffer more from the effects of the Rapture because it is more highly advanced technologically. Not that Americans are any better than anyone else on the planet, but, undoubtedly, key people in critical positions will be taken.

For example, a man responsible for maintaining a nuclear power plant's safety might disappear. A neurosurgeon might be performing a brain procedure when he suddenly vanishes. A pilot might be approaching JFK in New York or LAX at Los Angeles when the Rapture occurs.

A thousand scenarios could come to mind when thinking of the potential disasters.

Those who are left behind might eventually buy a lie that tells them it's all for the best that these people were gotten rid of, but one thing sure, those taken won't be forgotten. The disasters caused by their sudden disappearance will serve as monuments to them for months following the Rapture.

STRANGERS COULDN'T HAVE TAKEN 'EM ALL!

News media have recently chosen to make the abduction and murder of children a bandwagon cause. This is not to complain; it's a worthy thing to give publicity to those horror cases in order that the kids be recovered, and the beastly perpetrators be brought to justice.

But the cases of child abduction and murder are always with

our society. Media interest will fade, and a new bandwagon cause will emerge, onto which everybody will be led to jump.

One day, every infant, every young child will vanish from the Earth. This, in the view of many of us who are parents and grandparents, will perhaps be among the most significant catastrophes for those left behind.

These young ones will be taken in the Rapture by a loving God of perfect character, righteous in all His ways. How could a loving God take children and leave parents still on a chaotic Earth, separated from them? The answer is because children who have not reached the age when they know to make the decision to accept Jesus Christ as their Savior from sin are viewed by God as automatically righteous in His eyes. These, like all who have asked Christ into their lives to redeem them from sin, will be raptured.

These little ones are not to undergo the terrors of the Tribulation. That would be totally counter to the perfect character of God.

From the baby still in the mother's womb, to the oldest child who doesn't yet realize he must decide on Christ's sacrifice for humanity—all will be suddenly gone. This might be the most horrific of all aspects of the period on Earth that immediately follows the Rapture.

AFTER THE AFTERSHOCKS

Imagine the absolute bedlam that will dominate just America alone. Remember the worry, anxieties, and even terror, following the 9/11 attacks? The Rapture event will be that magnified thousands of times!

Government officials will at first find themselves unable to get a grip on the out-of-control situations that will be compounding by the minute. Many aftershocks will rumble across America and the world as key nuclear nations set their defenses for attacking whatever enemy is responsible for what has been happening. Time will lag, especially in some of the less communications-savvy countries, between the disappearances and the understanding that the catastrophes are global. Could it be out of the question that some nuclear exchanges might take place, before that realization is reached? Who knows for sure what measures are in place for automatically reacting to perceived attacks when human operators are incapacitated? It will likely take the hand of God to prevent mankind from launching nuclear war at that moment of utter confusion.

CALM, COOL, AND COLLECTED

Bible prophecy foretells that a time of relative peace will come upon the earthly scene before the Tribulation judgments begin. We can know, therefore, that the tremendous chaos that is the result of the Rapture will soon be dealt with to the degree that order is restored.

We have seen how quickly governmental actions were put together, recommended, then acted upon by Congress, the courts, and the executive branch in the U.S. following the 9/11 attacks. Even those who might normally oppose such things as rigid airport security checks, random police and military stops for security examinations, and increased surveillance methods for all private communications were willing to look the other way while these were implemented.

The term "homeland security" has become part of the American vernacular. It does, somehow, have a ring of some things we've heard about in totalitarian states, though, doesn't it? Still, it seems necessary. Government intrusion into our liberty and privacy seems infinitely better than a nuclear or biological weapon being exploded in a large population center.

So it will likely be after the Rapture. Any control method to regain order will probably be acceptable. There are people who will welcome the chance to institute such controls.

Everything and everyone will settle into the post-disappearance world. Then the explanations and rationalizations will begin. The propaganda machines will get fully in gear in preparation for that rider on the white horse of Revelation 6:1.

LEFT-BEHIND LITIGATION

Once the chaos settles, material possessions will have to be redistributed among families of those who are no longer there. Lawyers who are left behind after the Rapture will doubtless have overflowing numbers of cases to litigate.

Attorneys will think they've died and gone to Heaven.

The stock exchanges of the world will find new and profitable ways to operate. Insurance companies will rapidly adjust, but not before hashing out how to solve claims. Do companies have to pay for those who are suddenly missing? Are they dead, or not? Do the pre-disappearance laws and regulations apply to the life insurance industry? Does that mean those who have suddenly gone missing won't be declared legally dead for the prescribed legal period of time? How much interest can be gained from the monies that will have to be eventually paid out, if companies don't have to pay until the "legally dead" period has run its course?

You get the point. It will be, to put it mildly, an interesting time for the legal and financial worlds.

MEANWHILE, IN HEAVEN

In the heavenlies, things will be a million times more electrifying than on Earth, but in quite the opposite direction. People far below will sit bug-eyed in front of their TV screens, or stand staring in astonishment. We can only speculate, based upon Bible prophecy, what, at the same moment, will be going on with those who have heard the shout "Come up here!"

Face to Face

The movement from Earth to the Church's rendezvous with Christ will be instantaneous. We can know this, because Paul the apostle said that to be absent from the earthly body is to be present with the Lord (*Find It Fast:* 2 Corinthians 5:8).

All Church Age believers who have died and who are alive will find themselves looking their Savior and Lord in the face the moment Christ says "Come up here" (*Find It Fast:* Revelation 4:1). Every human sense will be accelerated and heightened. Those senses of sight, hearing, touch, smell, and speech will take on supernatural qualities at the moment of Rapture. Brainpower will increase infinitely. Those raptured will have abilities much like Christ's in every respect.

Again, we can know this because of what the Word of God says. John, the prophet and apostle, said: "Beloved, now we are children of God; and it has not yet been revealed what we shall be, but we know that when He is revealed, we shall be like Him, for we shall see Him as He is" (1 John 3:2).

Glorified Lord, Not Crucified Commoner

The eyes of the Jesus Christ into which the raptured believers will look will be those of deity. He is at this moment not the lowly babe of the manger or the child who was raised by the carpenter Joseph to become a carpenter. He is not the itinerate preacher, who at age thirty began preaching in the area we call the Holy Land. He is not even the great miracle worker who healed lepers, opened the eyes of the blind, got rid of a legion of demons, and raised the dead to life. He is now the King of all kings, to whom God the Father has given a name above every other name. He is the glorified Christ, who will judge every person who has ever lived. He is God, himself, before whom everyone will bow, according to the Bible.

Heavenly Homecoming

FIND IT FAST

While preparations for the salvation of Planet Earth are going on, those raptured will enter the city of God, Heaven. Although Revelation, chapter 22 gives some details about that place, also called the "New Jerusalem," we can't begin to speculate about the experience of entering Heaven. Our finite minds can't grasp such an infinite thing. All we can know about it is what the Bible tells us: "But as it is written: 'Eye has not seen, nor ear heard, nor have entered into the heart of man, the things which God has prepared for those who love him'" (1 Corinthians 2:9).

Fantastic Family Feast

Heaven will be celebrating when all of these things are being figured out on Earth. Bible prophecy has quite a bit to say about what will happen from the time of the Rapture through the earliest time when the Church is in Heaven.

RAPTURE AND BEYOND

1. **Church Age** (Acts 2:1–12) The time from the Holy Spirit coming to indwell believers to the Rapture (the present).
2. **Rapture** (1 Thessalonians 4:13–18; 1 Corinthians 15:51–55) Christ gathers the Church Age believers in the air.
3. **Judgment Seat of Christ, or Bema** (2 Corinthians 5:10)— Church Age believers are given rewards for their earthly deeds.
4. **Marriage Supper of the Lamb** (Revelation 19:7–9) Church Age believers are symbolically made the wife of Jesus Christ. Believers of times other than the Church Age are guests at this wedding.
5. **Return of Christ/Second Coming** (2 Thessalonians 1:7–10; Revelation 19:11–14) Christ returns with His Bride and all the heavenly hosts.
6. **Millennium** (Revelation 19:15–21; 20:1–3) Christ begins to rule His 1,000-year kingdom on Earth and binds Satan in chains for most of that time.
7. **Satan Unbound** (Revelation 20:7–10) Satan is unchained for a brief time at the end of the millennium and leads a rebellion with millions of people against Christ. Christ

instantly defeats Satan, who is then thrown into the Lake of Fire (Hell).

8. **Great White Throne Judgment** (Revelation 20:11–15) All unbelievers of all ages are individually judged for their unbelief. Each is then cast into the Lake of Fire (Hell) for eternity.

9. **God Makes All Things New** (Revelation 21:1) God recreates the Earth and the heavens, restoring them to perfection.

10. **Perfect Peace** (Revelation 21; 22:1–5) Believers live eternally in the presence of God in perfect joy and peace.

We have seen before that Jesus promised to come again for the Church (all who are born again). That rendezvous is found in John 14:1–3: "Let not your heart be troubled; you believe in God, believe also in me. In my Father's house are many mansions; if it were not so, I would have told you. I go to prepare a place for you. And if I go and prepare a place for you, I will come again and receive you to Myself; that where I am, there you may be also."

The Jewish bridegroom provided a dowry as payment for his bride. This was done in this symbolic marriage between Jesus and His Church, when He paid with His life to claim believers. The Church is His forever.

The bride of the Jewish tradition waited and watched for her beloved bridegroom to come for her. At an unannounced time, he would call the bride to come out from her home. She would join him, and they would set off for the home he had prepared for her.

The Church, in this analogy, accompanies their Lord into the Father's house—Heaven.

A Super Supper

The next thing that's prophesied to occur is the Marriage Supper of the Lamb. Again, the Church (all who have accepted Christ for their salvation during the Church Age) are likened to Christ's bride. The meeting somewhere above Earth with Jesus, then, is symbolic of the bride meeting her bridegroom, which is analogous to a Jewish marriage tradition. The bride is called out of her home, to meet the bridegroom. They then go to the place the groom has prepared for them to live.

The Scripture says in Luke 12:36 that Christ will return from a wedding. Prophecy foretells the marriage of Christ to believers: " 'Let us be glad and rejoice and give Him glory, for the marriage of the Lamb has come, and His wife has made herself ready.' And to her it was granted to be arrayed in fine linen, clean and bright, for the fine linen is the righteous acts of the saints" (Revelation 19: 7–8).

The Marriage Supper of the Lamb comes before the marriage itself. As with details about Heaven and all it encompasses, we can only imagine and speculate what is entailed when considering this event.

Jewish weddings of this tradition were joyful events, where a good time was had by all. That kind of good time, magnified by a factor of at least a million, might describe the exhilaration of the marriage between Christ and the Church.

The "Lamb," of course, is a reference to Jesus as the sacrificial Lamb who took away the sins of the world when He died on the cross at Calvary, was buried, and resurrected to newness of life— eternal life. The glorious Marriage Supper of the Lamb is in tremendous contrast to the dark, foreboding that life on Earth harbors.

BACK ON EARTH . . . LEFT-BEHIND LUNACY

Once things settle somewhat on Earth, strange, even weird activities are prophetically scheduled to begin taking place. Jesus, himself, gave the warning signs of that early time of the Tribulation.

MARK 13:21–23

Jesus said that many would come on the scene claiming to represent Him. They will even claim to be Him. But He warns those left behind not to believe that He, Christ, is present in the world at that time, because He won't be.

The "false christs" will deceive and delude with mystical performances of power and signs and wonders. But their power will not be from God. Jesus warns people, through the prophecy, to not let themselves be deceived by these satanically inspired activities.

A MAN GETS HIS WISH

The Holy Spirit, as we have seen, has been removed from His post of keeping a lid on evil. Now, evil is allowed to run amok, without much godly influence.

Man's government will try to bring all disorder under control.

Finally, those who want to govern themselves totally apart from God will get their chance to show what they can do. It will be as if God says to His creation, mankind: "Okay, you think you don't need me and that you can do a better job. Have at it."

But, where God's influence is suppressed, Satan's influence becomes stronger. He will begin to take over control of the planet. When God the Holy Spirit takes His hand off Earth to a large extent, weird things will begin to happen. Supernatural things.

Apparently, the supernatural aspects of the Tribulation era will increase greatly from this early point forward. Finally, a man called the "false prophet" will point deluded people of that time to the beast, Antichrist, as being the real Christ come to rescue the planet. The governments and power brokers of the Earth will give their power and authority to this political superman (*Find It Fast*: Revelation 17:12–13).

FIND
IT
FAST

Earth-Saving Solutions

Humanists will at last have their big chance to save the planet. They've strongly implied all along that God is dead—if indeed He ever existed. Now, in the time of Earth's greatest need for solutions, the globalist elitists will be able to formulate them.

As we've already brought up, a genius politician will step forward from among world leaders. Accounts of his prophesied time on Earth, as we've seen, are sprinkled throughout the Old and New Testaments. The account that best encapsulates his reign is found in Revelation, chapter 13.

REVELATION 13:1-2

John, the apostle and prophet, watched, in a vision, a strange beast emerge from the sea. It was unlike any animal on Earth. The creature had seven heads and ten horns. There was a crown upon each horn. Each head had upon it words that cursed God. The monster looked like a leopard, but had feet like a bear's, and a mouth like a lion's. Satan gave the beast his great power and authority.

All about the Beast

The weird composite beast seen here by John the apostle symbolizes preceding forms of world government, including the last world empire. (The beast and all it involves are covered in depth in Chapter 11, "Mr. 666.")

The great world leader will have many ideas that will, according to prophecy, amaze and thrill most everyone. It is, of course, speculation at this point, but it is easy to imagine a few things he will include in his plan for solving Earth's formidable problems.

Globalists have long wanted to redistribute wealth. This is so that the have-nots can have more. They proclaim this would cut down on the class envies, thus the wars. Probably, the world leader will include giving the wealth of those who disappeared to those left-behind people who deserve a better standard of living.

Forgiveness of debt will likely be another of his brilliant suggestions. Nations owing other countries should be forgiven debts owed to more fortunate creditor nations, he might encourage. This will show the spirit of love, unification, and cooperation, the great man will likely say.

The new world order under Antichrist when he comes to his full power, however, will offer only hate, destruction, and enslavement, according to Bible prophecy. Some people left behind will likely think they've died and gone to Heaven when they are allowed to take over the possessions of those who vanished. But those who have departed will have gladly traded all the material wealth of Planet Earth for their God-guaranteed heavenly rewards. So if you're not Rapture ready, and therefore left behind when the big event happens, you can have the house and car, with our blessings.

ONLY THE
DEAD CAN'T
SEND WEALTH
AHEAD!

CHAPTER 9

What about Your Heavenly Investments?

Rocketing over the Mediterranean in the middle of the night, Rayford had about a two hour flight to Greece . . .

When the Gulfstream was far enough out over the water, local radio tower signals faded, without satellite aid . . . He switched off phone and radio, which left him in virtual silence at thirty-one thousand feet in a smooth-as-silk jet, most of the noise of the craft behind him.

Rayford suddenly felt the weight of life. Had it really been a mere three and a half years ago that he had enjoyed the prestige, the ease, and the material comfort of the life of a 747 captain for a major airline? He'd been no prize, he knew, as a husband and father, but the cliché was true: You never know what you've got till it's gone.

Life since the Rapture, or what most of the world called the disappearances, had been different as night and day from before—and not just spiritually. Rayford likened it to a death in the family. Not a day passed when he didn't awaken under the burden of the present, facing the cold fact that though he had now made his peace with God, he had been left behind.

It was as if the whole nation, indeed the whole world, lived in suspended mourning and grief. Everyone had lost someone, and not a second could pass when one was able to forget that.

Tim LaHaye and Jerry Jenkins, *The Indwelling*
(Wheaton, Illinois: Tyndale, 2000)

EARTHLY WEALTH EVAPORATES

Midway through the Tribulation, Rayford Steele, one of the main characters of *The Indwelling,* realizes all earthly wealth is fleeting. It is insignificant, when compared to his wife and son, now in Heaven.

Earthly investments can't be counted on as a sure thing, as anyone who tries to keep up with the ups and downs, twists and turns, highs and lows of the stock market knows all too well. Eternal investments, however, are profitable to an unimaginable degree none of us can understand fully until our account is examined in the celestial city.

Investment Wisdom

The saying in Christian circles "Things of this life soon will be past; only things done for Christ will last" is as true as the Word of God itself. Things we do down here for God's kingdom are eternal and always build in value. This is because "Every good gift and every perfect gift is from above, and comes down from the Father of lights, with whom there is no variation or shadow of turning" (James 1:17).

The Lord is the same yesterday, today, and forever. Heavenly investments will never lose their value, because God is forever in charge of your account. So how does one invest in Heaven? Glad you asked . . .

GOD'S MYSTERIOUS MONEY MATTERS

FIND IT FAST

Paul related that man has very little understanding of the splendor that God is preparing for His faithful children (*Find It Fast:* 1 Corinthians 2:9). But that eternal wealth is not always obvious from our earthly vantage point. It is impossible to know exactly who is richer than someone else in the kingdom of God. Jesus indicated from the example of the widow's two mites (*Find It Fast:* Mark 12:42–44) that what is in the giver's heart is more important than what is in the giver's hand.

God's Economy

God's economic structure isn't like economies on Earth. If one man had a million dollars to his name and he gave $1,000 to God's work, his gift would be dwarfed by a man who lived in poverty and gave $20 to a ministry of God.

A good outward indication that a pastor is building up great treasure in Heaven might be his having a church that seats ten thousand people, a series of best-selling books, and a successful radio and TV ministry. But again, spiritual success can sometimes be hard to recognize.

Consider the case of Robert Morrison, the first Protestant missionary to China. He sailed into the port of Canton in 1807 and labored there twenty-seven years, until his death in 1834. During the entire span of Morrison's missionary career, he only baptized ten Chinese nationals. His pioneering work, which included a six-volume Chinese dictionary and a translation of the Bible, laid the foundation for other missionaries to build on. People whose focus is mainly on accumulating wealth might perceive Morrison to be a complete failure, but God surely judges otherwise.

GOD'S BILLIONAIRES

The world has its various rankings of wealthy individuals. *Forbes* magazine specializes in keeping a head count of who has achieved billionaire status. The number changes wildly with the ups and downs of the stock market, but currently the number stands at five hundred individuals with a net worth over the $1 billion mark. The kingdom of God has its own roster of heavenly billionaires. The following list is just a small representation of some noteworthy people who have achieved greatness.

⊕ **King David** God referred to David as a man after His own heart. David's historical legacy was his founding of the Judean dynasty. David won most of his greatest conquests on the battlefield. As a boy, he killed the godless giant Goliath, with just one stone from his slingshot. David was

God's greatest warrior; he defeated the Philistines, Moabites, Aramaeans, Ammonites, Edomites, and Amalekites. Both the Old Testament and New Testament include references to the Messiah as "the Son of David." David is credited with writing seventy-three of the Psalms.

⊕ **John the Baptist** Gauging the amount of heavenly wealth John achieved is not easy. John the Baptist did not write any books of the Bible, he had a very short ministry, and even his life was abbreviated. It wasn't until Jesus made His comments about John that we learned that he was a man of great riches. Jesus said: "Assuredly, I say to you, among those born of women there has not risen one greater than John the Baptist; but he who is least in the kingdom of heaven is greater than he" (Matthew 11:11).

⊕ **Apostle Paul** Most Christians cite Paul as the man who has done the most to advance Christianity. This is an amazing accomplishment for someone who first tried to destroy the Church that is now so greatly indebted to him. If heavenly wealth were determined by deeds alone, Paul would have an overwhelming lead over his fellow heroes of the faith.

Called the "apostle to the Gentiles," Paul probably holds the most patents in the field of missionary work. With the New Testament containing thirteen letters bearing his byline, there can be no doubt of his multibillionaire status. There can be little doubt, as well, that he is currently one of Heaven's most prominent citizens. He wrote almost half of the twenty-seven books in the New Testament and endured endless travail for the cause of Christ.

Anyone suffering from delusions of greatness needs to ponder Paul's record of faith. Paul wrote near the end of his life: "I have fought the good fight, I have finished the race, I have kept the faith. Finally, there is laid up for me the crown of righteousness, which the Lord, the righteous Judge, will give to me on that Day, and not to me only but also to all who have loved His appearing" (2 Timothy 4:7–8).

⊕ **Martin Luther** He made his fortune by setting the Reformation into motion. The grand opening event was held when Luther nailed his *Ninety-Five Theses* to the door of the Wittenberg Church. The document contained an attack on papal abuses and the sale of indulgences by church officials. He basically helped revive what has always been the heart of the Gospel—the principle that justification comes by faith alone. Luther became the father of a huge network of denominations that bear his name.

⊕ **John Bunyan** Probably the greatest Christian fiction writer of all time, Bunyan is most noted for his book *Pilgrim's Progress*. It has been said that his famous allegory about Pilgrim on his journey to the Celestial City is second only to the Bible itself in the number of copies sold through the ages and throughout the world. Bunyan was jailed many times for preaching the Gospel without an official license. This turned out to be a blessing in disguise, as Bunyan did some of his best writing in the jailhouse.

⊕ **John Wesley** Wesley was born in June 1703 in Epworth Rectory, England. He energetically and untiringly advanced the Gospel message. The Methodist movement was not an overnight success. He gained prosperity only through a long series of years, and amid some of the bitterest persecutions. In nearly every part of England, the movement was first met by rock-throwing mobs. The name "Methodist" came from the businesslike organizing power that the movement displayed. After Wesley's death, the Methodist Church grew into a huge denomination. Its success was guaranteed by military perfection instilled into its leadership by its founder.

⊕ **Charles Wesley** Some folks say that Charles Wesley was the first Methodist. He is noted as being the first one to bring together a group of like-minded believers in the "Holy Club" at Oxford. Leadership was not Charles's specialty; he normally turned executive matters over to his brother John. Charles's main calling, and the source of much of his eternal wealth, was the hundreds of hymns he wrote. You don't need to attend a Methodist service to hear them. His hymns have become standards of most Christian denominations.

⊕ **Charles Haddon Spurgeon** Spurgeon stands as one of England's best-known church leaders. Greatly blessed by the Holy Spirit, he was only twenty years old when he became the pastor of a small London church. His congregation grew so large that the church had to move several times before it finally found a location large enough. Spurgeon frequently preached to more than ten thousand, and this was before microphones and speakers. His ability to thoroughly relate biblical messages to the common person was, many believe, the secret to his success. Spurgeon's many writings and sermons are still widely published.

⊕ **William Booth** During the 1800s, there must have been something special in Britain's water because here we have yet another native of England who founded a prosperous global Christian organization. Booth was an evangelist in London, where he and his wife, Catherine, established "the Christian Mission" to address the evangelical and social-welfare needs of the inhabitants of the slums of London. In

1878, the Mission was reorganized along its present quasi-military lines and was renamed the Salvation Army. Today, the group has become one of the largest charitable organizations in the world.

INFAMOUS FINANCIAL FIASCOES

Over the years, the financial world has experienced a number of infamous financial fiascoes. The spiritual realm has had several financial disasters of its own. Nothing can be more tragic than for someone to have the opportunity to achieve eternal greatness and then lose it because of his own fraud or neglect.

⊕ **Judas Iscariot** If anyone had the promise of great wealth, it was Judas Iscariot. The Bible says that the names of the twelve apostles will be inscribed into the twelve foundations of Heaven (*Find It Fast:* Revelation 21:14). Jesus said the twelve disciples will also sit on twelve thrones judging the nations of Israel. Judas saw the miracles and he walked with Jesus all that time, but still somehow he failed to see the eternal riches that were being placed in his name. We all know he sold everything that could have been his for a meager payment of thirty pieces of silver.

⊕ **Asa Alonzo Allen** A. A. Allen stands, perhaps, as the saddest story of a preacher turned charlatan. He is most well known for telling his followers that he could command God to turn dollar bills into twenties. Allen claimed to be anointed with the power to make wealthy those who gave $100 to his ministry. He also urged his followers to send for his prayer cloths anointed with miracle oil, and he offered "miracle tent shavings" as points of contact for personal miracles. Allen was kicked out of the Assemblies of God denomination when he jumped bail after being arrested for drunk driving. He claimed that the drunk driving offense resulted from him being kidnapped and having alcohol forcefully poured down his throat by some thugs. On June 14, 1970, listeners were hearing this recorded message from A. A. Allen on his radio program: "This is Brother Allen in person. Numbers of friends of mine have been inquiring about reports they have heard concerning me that are not true. People, as well as some preachers from pulpits, are announcing that I am dead. Do I sound like a dead man? My friends, I am not even sick! Only a moment ago I made a reservation to fly into our current campaign. I'll see you there and make the devil a liar." At that moment, at the Jack Tar Hotel in San Francisco, police were removing A. A. Allen's body from a room littered with pills and empty liquor bottles. Allen died from liver failure brought about by acute alcoholism (James Randi, *The Faith Healers*, Prometheus Books, 1989, p. 88).

⊕ **Robert Tilton** From the very beginning, the sole purpose of the Robert Tilton Ministry was apparently to extract money from believers. Tilton got the inspiration for starting "Success-N-Life" from watching Dave Del Dotto's real estate infomercials. Tilton's love of earthly wealth is so prevalent that it even shows in his own personal testimony. He chose to go to a Hawaiian resort to get saved because, in his words, "If I'm going to go to the cross, I'm going to go in a pretty place. Not some dusty place like Jerusalem. Gravel is all that place is" (Scott Baradell, "Robert Tilton's Heart of Darkness," *Dallas Observer,* February 6, 1992, 19–20). Tilton built an empire that, at its peak, took in as much as $65 million per year. The end came when an ABC news program found out that the prayer request letters he promised to pray over were being trashed unread. All of Tilton's mail was sent directly to his Tulsa bank; the checks were removed and deposited, and the prayer requests were thrown in Dumpsters. A reporter, while digging through the garbage, found desperate requests for things like healing of heart and eye conditions. Tilton's operation dwindled rapidly amid the revelations of the scandal. In his defense, Tilton said the prayer requests were planted, and he also said, "I laid on top of those prayer requests so much that the chemicals actually got into my bloodstream, and . . . I had two small strokes in my brain" (Robert Tilton, "Success-N-Life," November 22, 1991).

⊕ **Jim Bakker and PTL** Disclosure of the gross overbooking of time-shares at Jim Bakker's Christian theme park forced it into bankruptcy. The "Praise The Lord" satellite network was eventually doomed to obscurity by the circus that enveloped the ministry. After being tried and convicted of fraud, Bakker went to prison for several years. He's now out of prison and last report has him serving a small congregation of people—his once vast media empire a distant memory.

EXPLODING PROSPERITY

A recent World Wealth Report created by Merrill Lynch and Cap Gemini Ernst & Young found the global net worth of all equity and real estate amounted to a massive $26.2 trillion. In the U.S., the number stands at around $13 trillion. The longest economic boom in history has helped create a vast pool of prosperity.

Money Hungry

Men work endlessly to grow their portfolios, but for what purpose? A man with $10 billion is just as overwhelmingly rich as someone who has $20 billion. Far too many people think they're poor because someone else has more money than they.

Unless you put money to some use, it really doesn't have any value. In fact, value is mostly created by the act of hoarding money. If everyone suddenly decided to sell all the stocks they own, wealth based on equity prices would instantly collapse. In the end, a rich person is not someone who has money; a rich person is someone who uses money.

To be truly rich in the eternal sense, you need to be investing your money in the kingdom of God. In this area, people of earthly wealth fail miserably.

One survey by the Barna Research Group found that people in the most affluent income level only tithe about 5 percent of their earnings to religious charities. Wealthy celebrities rank even lower. One site that reviewed the tax returns of a number of well-known Hollywood personalities could not find one celebrity who gave money to a Gospel-minded organization.

Philanthropic Foolishness

When the rich finally do decide to give away a portion of their fortune, AIDS causes, libraries, secular colleges, museums, and medical research are some of the typical recipients of their donations. It's ironic that people can be wise enough to build up large sums of money through earthly investments and then end up putting it all into temporary things of this life while completely ignoring heavenly investments.

Scrooge Lives!

Probably one of the best descriptions of what the afterlife will be like for men of great wealth can be found in Charles Dickens's *A Christmas Carol*. The torment of men like Jacob Marley, Scrooge's departed business partner, was not that he and others were weighted down with giant chains; their torment was that they could see the need in the world, but they could no longer "interfere, for good, in human matters."

Jesus said, "It is easier for a camel to go through the eye of a needle than for a rich man to enter into the kingdom of God" (Matthew 19:24).

Unloading Burden of Wealth

Rich people can take action to overcome the danger to their souls as warned about by Jesus. Simply because so few rich people give to the cause of Christ, someone well off could easily overcome the burden of wealth by giving to God.

There is a factor that might be called "the rich man's mite." If someone like Bill Gates decided to give a generous portion of his holdings to something like missionary work, even though he would have plenty of money left over, God would undoubtedly regard that person as giving in a measure equal to the widow in Mark 12:42.

Convenient Excuses

Some people refuse to do anything for the Lord's work because they claim they have doubts about their own motivation. These say they don't want to be guilty of doing something only so they'll get the honor and glory for doing it. When one gives or does something in Christ's name, nothing is wrong with a healthy expectancy of some future reward. It's true that personal gain should not be our only motivation, but such excuses as mentioned above can, themselves, bring guilt that is just as bad.

Ever-Mindful Motivation

What should keep Christians going is the realization that someday Jesus is going to demand to know what good we've all done in our lives. Paul wrote: "Knowing, therefore, the terror of the Lord, we persuade men . . ." (2 Corinthians 5:11). It is the wise person who realizes he or she needs all the points he or she can muster!

MAKING FINANCIAL PLANS

If the Bible promised a full week's warning before the Rapture takes place, most churches would almost certainly be full the Sunday preceding the great event. Because of the huge bounty of giving, the ushers would probably have to go down the aisles using wheelbarrows to gather the offering. Of course, all the money given at the last minute would be nearly worthless.

Parting with Prosperity?

When the Rapture takes place, all the assets we have in banks and brokerages will indeed be worthless. As they pass into glory, some people whom God greatly blessed in this life might have to endure a dramatic reduction in their prosperity level.

A study by the Vanguard Group found that 49 percent of all private sector salaried and waged workers have a long-term investment plan to which they regularly contribute. When you include savings plans of federal employees, the number goes up to 60 percent of the population. We've already stated that the number of people who have eternally minded investment plans is in the single-digit percentile.

Prosperity Message

Giving tithes and offerings to various ministries is often motivated by what is commonly called the "prosperity gospel," which states that if you give God $100, He'll give you back $1,000, or maybe even $10,000. With time likely being so short, and with the valuations of this life so temporal, it's prudent to ask the Lord to just keep the money in the heavenly realm.

Jesus said: "Do not store up for yourselves treasures on earth, where moth and rust destroy, and where thieves break in and steal. But store up for yourselves treasures in Heaven, where moth and rust do not destroy, and where thieves do not break in and steal. For where your treasure is, there your heart will be also" (Matthew 6:19–21, New International Version).

MUCH MORE THAN JUST MONEY!

It's not just money we're talking about here. Souls are the most precious of all commodities on Earth and in Heaven. You can cut out the middleman by witnessing to people yourself. The reward for winning a new convert to Christ is priceless. If you get someone saved, you could pretty much take the rest of the month off. "He who wins souls is wise" (Proverbs 11:30).

Most faithful Christians look forward to Christ's return. If it was made known to us the current balance of our eternal reward, many believers who were once so eager to see Jesus return might instead be motivated to ask Him for an extension so our heavenly accounts could be nourished for eternity. Prophetic signals in our time forewarn that, ready or not, Jesus might come soon. Perhaps today!

MONEY: THE HEART OF THE MATTER

What is money? It comes in a wide variety of forms, but it has two main purposes. First, it is a means of exchange for goods and services. If a farmer had a dozen head of cattle on his ranch and he wanted to use them to buy a truck from a dealership, the salesman wouldn't normally take the farmer's herd of cattle for payment. The farmer would obviously take old Bessy and her companions to market and sell them for currency that he could use to purchase the vehicle.

Second, money measures the value of something. A painting by Leonardo da Vinci is esteemed according to the number of dollars a buyer is willing to pay for it.

People often make the mistake of measuring money by itself to determine value. This is why some wealthy people endure lives of self-inflicted poverty. To them, money is worth more than the basic necessities of life.

Money as Measure

An overwhelming number of people measure their own worth by how much money they have in the bank. If one man has $50,000 to his name and another man has $100,000 stashed away, it's common for people to think the second individual has double the reason to be content.

One of the most troublesome misconceptions people have about money is the belief that if we only had enough of it, all our problems would be resolved. Wealth can end financial troubles, but it can only provide distraction from all other difficulties. Someone once said, "Life is tragic for the person who has plenty to live on but nothing to live for."

Eternal Mistakes

The most important choice people can make in life is the decision to accept Jesus Christ as their personal Savior. People are responsible enough to make sure their life insurance policies are paid up, but a great number of them will fail to ensure the destination of their eternal souls. Not until after the unbelievers die do they realize what a tragic mistake they've made. Jesus said: "For what profit is it to a man if he gains the whole world, and loses his own soul? Or what will a man give in exchange for his soul?" (Matthew 16:26).

Rewards Unrealized

Christians are also facing a tragedy of great magnitude. Although it comes nowhere close to the sadness of someone losing out on eternal life, most Christians will end up missing out on a host of rewards the Lord promised He would give generously to His faithful servants.

After choosing to make Jesus the Lord of their life, too many Christians refuse to become actively involved in their faith. They neglect to realize there are levels of rewards in Heaven that relate directly to good deeds performed in this life. Jesus said the reward for sacrifice and commendable stewardship would be as high as a hundredfold return:

"And everyone who has left houses or brothers or sisters or father or mother or wife or children or lands, for My name's sake, shall receive a hundredfold, and inherit eternal life" (Matthew 19:29). Again, He said: "But he who received seed on the good ground is he who hears the word and understands it; who indeed bears fruit and produces: some a hundredfold, some sixty, some thirty" (Matthew 13:23).

IT'S ALL OVER!

When believers leave this earthly abode, they instantly lose the ability to make any improvements to their eternal standing. It's fascinating to ponder whether saints a thousand years from now will still be kicking themselves for not being more active in striving after God's favor.

The Centers for Disease Control says current life expectancy for the average American man is seventy-three years, up from forty-six years at the turn of the last century. Even with the improvement in life expectancy, our visit here is brief by any comparison to the vast expanse of time.

The Bible makes numerous references to the brevity of our earthly life. We are depicted as grass and flowers that are here today and gone tomorrow: "All flesh is as grass, and all the glory of man as

the flower of grass. The grass withers, and its flower falls away . . ."
(1 Peter 1:24).

Because we have no lasting foothold on Earth, it is essential that
we make plans for the life to come. A person once said, "There are
no pre-built mansions in Heaven. Every time we do something that
glorifies God's name the angels add one more brick to our eternal
dwelling place."

Master Craftsman at Work

Just before Jesus departed from the disciples, He told them that He
was going to prepare a place for them. He's been working on
Heaven for nearly two thousand years, so by now it must be quite a
spectacular place.

YOU LOSE WHAT YOU KEEP

George W. Truett, a well-known pastor, was invited to dinner in the
home of a very wealthy man in Texas. After the meal, the host led
him to a place where they could get a good view of the surrounding
area.

Pointing to the oil wells punctuating the landscape, he boasted,
"Twenty-five years ago I had nothing. Now, as far as you can see, it's
all mine." Looking in the opposite direction, at his sprawling fields
of grain, he said, "That's all mine." Turning east toward huge herds
of cattle, he bragged, "They're all mine." Then pointing to the west
and a beautiful forest, he exclaimed, "That too is all mine."

He paused, expecting Dr. Truett to compliment him on his

HEAVEN'S TREASURE TROVE

The kingdom of Heaven is like a multibillionaire who decides to give away his wealth to all comers, and only a few people show up to receive the bounty.

F. E. Marsh has compiled a list of some of God's blessings that await the faithful:

⊕ an acceptance that can never be questioned (Ephesians 1:6)
⊕ an inheritance that can never be lost (1 Peter 1:3–5)
⊕ a deliverance that can never be excelled (2 Corinthians 1:10)
⊕ a grace that can never be limited (2 Corinthians 12:9)
⊕ a hope that can never be disappointed (Hebrews 6:18, 19)
⊕ a bounty that can never be withdrawn (Colossians 3:21–23)
⊕ a joy that need never be diminished (John 15:11)
⊕ a nearness to God that can never be reversed (Ephesians 2:13)
⊕ a peace that can never be disturbed (John 14:27)
⊕ a righteousness that can never be tarnished (2 Corinthians 5:21)

great success. Truett, however, placing one hand on the man's shoulder and pointing heavenward with the other, simply said, "How much do you have in that direction?"

The Rapture can take place at any moment. What about your heavenly investments?

IT'S NOT
TOO LATE
UNLESS
YOU WAIT!

CHAPTER 10

Oops, I Guess I Wasn't Ready!

Rayford lay there grieving, knowing the television would be full of scenes he didn't want to see, dedicated around the clock to the tragedy and mayhem all over the world. And then it hit him.

He sat up, staring out the window in the darkness. He owed it to Chloe not to fail her. He loved her and she was all he had left. He had to find out how they had missed everything Irene had been trying to tell them, why it had been so hard to accept and believe. Above all, he had to study, to learn, to be prepared for whatever happened next.

If the disappearances were of God, if they had been his doing, was this the end of it? . . .

. . . If there was still a way to find the truth and believe or accept or whatever it was Irene said one was supposed to do, Rayford was going to find it . . .

—*Left Behind*

A DREADFUL DILEMMA

Realization that he is alone slams hard into the pilot's fatigued brain. Left behind in the disappearance catastrophe, Rayford Steele grieves for the loss of his wife and son. Millions will be in similar dilemmas following the Rapture. Although explanations and theories will be flying through the electronic airwaves, each person left behind will sense for a time the God he or she never paid much attention to before has rejected him or her.

We'll spend some time here looking more closely at the days immediately following the vanishing. What will be the thoughts, the actions, the fears and hopes of those who were not taken? The Bible provides explanation, warning, comfort, and advice for that most troubled era in human history.

FOR THOSE WHO WEREN'T READY

Our focus here will be primarily on those of you who have found this chapter after the Rapture. However, we highly recommend that if you are reading this before the Pre-Tribulation Rapture, you think about the negative consequences of being left behind. Seriously consider committing your life to Jesus, if you haven't already.

WHAT'S HAPPENED?

Right now, there's a tremendous battle going on, with various points of view trying to explain why millions of people just suddenly vanished into thin air. It's likely that the media are teeming with possible explanations for the disappearances. It would be foolish to try to guess what authorities will be telling the general population right after it happens.

SNATCHING IS SUPERNATURAL

We boldly say from this side of that event, however, that the cause was supernatural. The mass disappearance of all those people was the result of the Lord Jesus Christ removing from the Earth all who were spiritually ready. This catching up of the Christians into Heaven is referred to as the Rapture of the Church, which, as we've presented earlier in this book, is detailed in the following Bible prophecies of the Pre-Tribulation event:

- ⊕ "For the Lord Himself will descend from heaven with a shout, with the voice of an archangel, and with the trumpet of God. And the dead in Christ will rise first. Then we who are alive and remain shall be caught up together with them in the clouds to meet the Lord in the air. And thus we shall always be with the Lord. Therefore comfort one another with these words" (1 Thessalonians 4:16–18).
- ⊕ "Behold, I tell you a mystery: We shall not all sleep, but we shall all be changed—in a moment, in the twinkling of an eye, at the last trumpet. For the trumpet will sound, and the dead will be raised incorruptible, and we shall be changed. For this corruptible must put on incorruption, and this mortal must put on immortality" (1 Corinthians 15:51–53).

WHY DIDN'T HE TAKE ME?

If you are reading this after the Rapture, you need to realize that you have been left behind. You may be feeling rejected by God at this time. You might be saying to yourself, "Why didn't He take me?" or "I don't understand; I've led a good life."

The problem isn't that God rejected you; the problem is that you have rejected Him. By not committing your life to Jesus, by not following after Him, you left Him with no other choice but to leave you behind.

⊕ "Not everyone who says to Me, 'Lord, Lord,' shall enter the kingdom of heaven, but he who does the will of My Father in heaven" (Matthew 7:21).

⊕ "For whoever does the will of My Father in heaven is My brother and sister and mother" (Matthew 12:50).

⊕ "'Come now, and let us reason together,' says the Lord. 'Though your sins are like scarlet, they shall be as white as snow; though they are red like crimson, they shall be as wool'" (Isaiah 1:18).

Is There Hope for Me?

Depending on how early you read this article, you may have heard people say, "Because we've missed the Rapture, we are lost forever." That assumption is totally wrong! The only way you can find yourself eternally lost is by receiving the mark of the beast on your right hand or forehead. Barring that, as long as you have breath in your lungs, you can gain salvation by trusting in Jesus Christ as your Savior.

⊕ "The one who comes to Me I will by no means cast out" (John 6:37).

⊕ "Come to Me, all you who labor and are heavy laden, and I will give you rest" (Matthew 11:28).

⊕ "But as many as received Him, to them He gave the right to become children of God, to those who believe in His name" (John 1:12).

Huge Crop of Saints

According to Revelation, there will be a huge number of people saved during the Tribulation. "After these things I looked, and behold, a great multitude which no one could number, of all nations, tribes, peoples, and tongues, standing before the throne and before the Lamb, clothed with white robes . . ." (Revelation 7:9). Some scholars have predicted that the number of Tribulation believers will grow to eclipse that of the saints—or Pre-Tribulation believers—who were raptured.

WHY DO I NEED JESUS CHRIST TO BE MY SAVIOR?

To be allowed to pass through Heaven's gate, you need to have all of your sins removed, and the only cleanser strong enough to thoroughly remove sin stains is the blood of Jesus Christ.

Everybody Needs a Bath

You could say Heaven is much like the "clean rooms" where computer companies make their microchips, and sin is like any dust or dirt that might try to find its way into one of those rooms. The manufacturing process for microchips requires "clean rooms" to be absolutely spotless, having virtually zero free-floating dust or dirt particles that could damage the delicate microchips.

Because humans are naturally contaminated with all kinds of dirt and dust particles, whenever workers enter one of these "clean rooms," they need to wear a special suit that prevents them from giving off particles.

Jesus Provides Cleansing Shower

To prevent Heaven from becoming contaminated with sin particles, God has long set the requirement that anyone desiring to enter into His untarnished dwelling place needs to be covered by the blood of Jesus.

The sin decontamination process is very simple—you simply ask Jesus Christ, the Son of God, for it. First, admit your sinful state. Next, ask Jesus to forgive you of your wrongdoings. Finally, make Jesus Christ Lord of your life by surrendering your will to Him.

Full Pardon

Jesus, by dying on the cross, has made it possible for each of us to be granted a full pardon from the punishment of eternal damnation.

The reason so few people accept this pardon is that they don't think they need a savior or they want to find their own way of salvation.

⊕ "Then Jesus said to His disciples, 'If anyone desires to come after Me, let him deny himself, and take up his cross, and follow Me. For whoever desires to save his life will lose it, but whoever loses his life for My sake will find it. For what profit is it to a man if he gains the whole world, and loses his own soul? Or what will a man give in exchange for his soul?'" (Matthew 16:24–26).

⊕ "If you confess with your mouth the Lord Jesus and believe in your heart that God has raised Him from the dead, you will be saved" (Romans 10:9–10).

⊕ "For God so loved the world that He gave His only begotten Son, that whoever believes in Him should not perish but have eternal life" (John 3:16).

CHANGING YOUR DIRECTION

After making Jesus the Lord of your life, you need to change the direction of your life. When on vacation, traveling in an unfamiliar place, people often make a wrong turn somewhere along the line. At some point, they realize they are lost. A spirited debate might ensue about which direction is the correct one. They have to then turn around and head in the right direction. So it is with the salvation process.

Once you realize you have been heading in the wrong direction, the only option that makes sense is to turn right around and start heading in the right direction. You can't just mouth a few words, and then continue on your same merry way. You must believe and accept with all your heart that Jesus is the way. You need to then make a full commitment to Jesus Christ by reading His words and following His examples of holy living.

"Enter by the narrow gate; for wide is the gate and broad is the way that leads to destruction, and there are many who go in by it. Because narrow is the gate and difficult is the way which leads to life, and there are few who find it" (Matthew 7:13–14).

BE DEDICATED OR DECEIVED

Every church on the planet will likely be filled to capacity on the Sunday immediately following the Rapture. Suddenly, everyone left behind will discover a need to renew his or her faith.

Unfortunately, the revival is going to be very short-lived. The Apostle Paul, in Thessalonians, predicts that because most people's hearts will still love unholy living, they will turn and follow after a deception that God himself will allow to come upon those who have rejected Him. Jesus foretold that the false prophets would arise using "great signs and wonders" to trick people into believing satanic lies.

There will be no middle ground. The people who failed to fully dedicate their lives to Christ will fall for the demonic delusion that will sweep over the world.

> ⊕ ". . . and with all unrighteous deception among those who perish, because they did not receive the love of truth, that they might be saved. And for this reason God will send them strong delusion, that they should believe the lie, that they all may be condemned who did not believe the truth but had pleasure in unrighteousness" (2 Thessalonians 2:10–12).

⊕ "For false christs and false prophets will rise and show great signs and wonders to deceive, if possible, even the elect" (Matthew 24:24).

Lying Leader

During the first few years after the Rapture, a world leader the Bible calls the Antichrist will arise. At first he will seem like the most benevolent leader that has ever held office. However, by the end of the Tribulation, his evil doings will easily put the horrendous deeds of past evil dictators to shame.

Only Believe the Bible

Because the lies of the Antichrist and false prophets will be so pervasive, you will need to assume that everything and anything in the mass media is tainted. Your exclusive source for the truth must now be the Bible.

In the coming days, you are going to see and hear messages from some of the biggest names in Christianity on radio and TV. These messages won't be ones recorded before the Rapture. The broadcasts you'll be hearing will be either live or taped afterward. They will be from so-called Christian leaders who, like you, have been left behind.

Millions of people will be reassured by the fact that their favorite Christian celebrities are still here. Expect most of these well-known leaders, possibly out of embarrassment, to be working feverishly to disprove the Rapture event. They may say that while they don't know where or why the people disappeared, they do know that it wasn't the so-called Rapture of the Church.

Pre-Trib Pretenders

It will be quite confusing to hear some people who were once re-
garded as the leading authorities on the Pre-Tribulation Rapture now
proclaiming contradictory theories. Don't listen to them, no matter
how well respected they appear. Listen only to those who are saying:
"Accept Jesus Christ, alone, and follow Him, even to the point of martyrdom."

Many religious and political leaders will be attempting to persuade you into believing some logical explanation for the Rapture.
All of their lies will be contrary to the Word of God. If they cause
you any doubt, just remember they were left behind just like you.
What business do they have instructing you?

Enduring to the End

Well, folks, here comes the unpleasant news. Most of you will likely
have to choose martyrdom if you wish to maintain your commitment to Jesus Christ. There will be no middle ground. During this
Tribulation hour, you will have to choose between two masters—the
Antichrist or Jesus Christ.

Your decision to follow Jesus will not be a popular one. The majority of the world's population will soon be falling captive to the
Antichrist's hypnotic words. Because true believers will refuse to join
the chorus of praise, the Antichrist will demand that all noncon-
forming Christians be put to death.

"It was granted to him to make war with the saints and to overcome them. And authority was given him over every tribe, tongue,
and nation. All who dwell on the earth will worship him, whose

names have not been written in the Book of Life of the Lamb slain from the foundation of the world. If anyone has an ear, let him hear. He who leads into captivity shall go into captivity; he who kills with the sword must be killed with the sword. Here is the patience and the faith of the saints" (Revelation 13:7–10).

"When he opened the fifth seal, I saw under the altar the souls of those who had been slain for the word of God and for the testimony which they held. And they cried with a loud voice, saying, 'How long, O Lord, holy and true, until You judge and avenge our blood on those who dwell on the earth?' Then a white robe was given to each of them; and it was said to them that they should rest a little while longer, until both the number of their fellow servants and their brethren, who would be killed as they were, was completed" (Revelation 6:9–11).

Choose to Miss the Mark

At first it may seem rather easy to secretly be a follower of Jesus Christ. Unfortunately, very soon the Antichrist will be requiring everyone to receive a mark in his or her right hand or forehead. This electronic implant will be the means by which everyone buys and sells goods and services. Members and leaders of the Antichrist regime will quickly know if you don't have this implant: ". . . and that no one may buy or sell except one who has the mark or the name of the beast, or the number of his name" (Revelation 13:17).

Because the Bible says that everyone who receives this implant ("mark of the beast") will be eternally lost, you are hereby highly advised to decline the offer when the government informs you that they have your implant ready for insertion. "And the smoke of their torment ascends forever and ever; and they have no rest day or night, who worship the beast and his image, and whoever receives the mark of his name" (Revelation 14:11).

Worst of Times!

During the coming persecution, you will be faced with the worst trials that Christians have ever had to endure. Yet you will know how long you will have to endure: From the time the Antichrist declares himself to be God, there will be only 1,260 days until Christ returns to Earth. He will then judge the nations and set up his Millennial Kingdom (*Find It Fast:* Daniel 12:11, Revelation 11:3). Your desire to see Christ should grow stronger as time passes, and the sufferings of the Tribulation grow more severe.

FIND
IT
FAST

Best of Times on the Way!

Scripture strongly indicates that most Tribulation saints will not live to see the end of the Tribulation. If you do find yourself facing a situation that requires you to lay down your life, God's Word promises you that your brief moment of pain will be nothing compared to the pleasures of an eternity in God's glory.

"And you will be hated by all for My name's sake. But he who endures to the end will be saved" (Matthew 10:22).

LEFT-BEHIND LETTERS

What could possibly be more terrifying than to suddenly realize God has supernaturally removed His true believers from the surface of the Earth, and for whatever reason, He has found you unprepared to enter into His kingdom?

The following words were written by Christians to help instruct, encourage, and guide you through what will soon become some very difficult and dark days. But, before you do anything, remember, you first need to fully turn your life over to Jesus Christ.

Dear Friend,

Are you looking for me? Is the world looking for millions of missing people who have just vanished in an instant? Are all little children around the globe part of the missing group? If so, I can tell you what has happened. Don't believe the very convincing lies you will hear. Don't believe that UFOs got us. Don't believe some cosmic reaction erased us. The truth is—are you ready for this?— we're at a wedding. Yup. In fact, we are the "bride." The "groom" is Jesus, the Messiah, the Promised One from the God of Abraham, Isaac, and Jacob. (Hear, O Israel!) He has come to take His bride, the true Church and all little innocent ones, out of this world because of what is coming. Yes, yes, I know. There are all sorts of "Christians" running around now insisting that this explanation cannot be the correct one because they are left behind. This may include some very visible Christians, including a number of internationally applauded Christian leaders. What does this tell you? It tells you that any "Christian" left behind was a phony. They may have said they believed, blah blah blah, but God knows the hearts of men, and he has seen that they are fakes.

Will you ever see us again? Will you ever see your loved ones who are missing? That's up to you. You see, Jesus has removed His bride from the Earth in one last attempt to get your attention. Are you paying attention now? Good! . . .

Read the last book of the Bible, Revelation. Read, in the Old Testament, the books Zechariah, Ezekiel, and Daniel. Look for anything that will help you get an understanding of what has happened. For example, you might find a set of books called the Left Behind *series by Tim LaHaye and Jerry Jenkins. Go to the homes of missing people and search their bookshelves. Go to churches that have lost most of their members and search the pastors' offices and church libraries for videotapes or study guides.*

Look for the Web sites of places like Jews for Jesus, Lamb and Lion Ministries, and others. Check out the "Rapture ready" sites that give tips on how to survive the Tribulation . . . True believers were taken out to spare them this time. It is not too late to be saved, and be assured that even if you do not physically survive to see Christ come again, you will go to Heaven at your death to wait with us. We will all return with Him at His glorious appearance! The honeymoon trip, you know. Now, adios! Having a wonderful time! Wish, truly, that you were here!!
—Herbert

Dear Friend:
I'm sure you're terrified and confused by all of the terrible events that have occurred. I'm sure you have heard the Rapture

theories by now, and you may wonder why I'm gone and you're here . . .

The Bible says that all *have sinned and fallen short of the glory of God, and it's so true. You've heard the old joke: "God, today I haven't cursed, cheated, lied, or hurt my fellow man. I haven't become impatient, greedy, or selfish. But I'm about to get up today, and I'm going to need your help!"*

I know you as well as I know myself. I grew up in a terrible family, where I was physically and emotionally abused by people who claimed to be Christians. It took me years to understand that people can say they are anything, but the proof is in their actions. Look around you. Are the phonies still around?

Of course . . .

God loves you so much, He wants to take care of you, if only you'll let Him! My life has gotten so much better since I turned my life over to God. It's been difficult at times but God always is there for me. I've never been hungry, or homeless, or hopeless once I put my faith in Him. Please! Read the page on getting saved, and what you need to do now. Ask God to show you His love, and He will.

—Your friend in Christ,
    Heather

Dear Family, Friends, and other Lost Sheep of the human race left behind:

If you're reading this, then I've left you behind to fend for yourselves. I'm sorry I failed you. I'm sorry I didn't do more to spread God's Word to you, or to demonstrate the truth of it by example in the way I lived my life. But I've always been weak, and a sinner. I'm the first to admit I was never perfect.

My quick temper, my greedy collecting of material things during my life, my laziness. Oh sure, there were times when I tried to live more by Jesus' example, but most often it ended in failure because of my own arrogance, pride, or stupidity. I've failed so many times. I've only managed to survive this long because I prayed to Jesus and to God to help me find the strength and wisdom to become a better person. I know I never did anything to deserve their love, but somehow through faith it found me. As you read this letter, I hope I can give you the encouragement to find it too, so that you too might be saved . . .

Nothing I can say or do can force you to believe in God or Jesus. Like so many things in life, it's just one of those truths that has to reveal itself to you over time, if you are open to it. It's a common saying that people can't accept the truth when it's dictated to them, and that the only thing that makes the truth palatable is the thrill of self-discovery.

So don't look to prophets, preachers, miracles, or rituals for proof. Don't spend so much effort looking for scientific or physical proof, but rather look to your own human experience, and deep within your own soul. Somewhere inside you, deep within, you eventually will come to know [through insights given you by God, the Holy Spirit] with all certainty the truth behind the teachings in the Bible . . .

I apologize if I have offended you for the tone of my letter being instructional in a bossy sort of way. I don't pretend to have all the answers, because even where I am now I am sure that I am learning every day. If you have found your way to my letter, then you must be somewhat open-minded to have come this far. If you can go a little farther then perhaps we will meet again. I love you. I miss you and pray for you every day. If there is any task I can endure to help you in your journey, then I ask Him to

*let me be there for you. Although my own heart and soul are
weak, through His love you can be saved.*
   Sincerely,
   Mark

To whom it may concern:
   *Well, this should concern everyone. By now you've probably
heard, thousands of people are gone, disappeared into thin air.
You might be afraid, and if so keep reading, I'd like to help you
to understand what is going on, the best that I can. However, I
am particularly concerned about those of you who do know. You
probably belonged to a church that taught you that once you said
those few words you had fire insurance and a sure spot in the
Rapture, no matter how you lived from that point on. You may
have been taught that there was no Rapture, it passed, it is still to
come, or that the world will be restored to paradise when Jesus
comes again.*
   *You now know the truth. The Rapture was real, it happened,
and you've been left behind . . .*
   *This is no time for "I told you so," because the time is short.
Your first step is to pray. I don't know for sure what will happen
in your future, but I have been told that there will be saints
coming out of the Rapture. You can be one of them. Pray, receive
Christ into your heart now, for real, tell Him that no matter
what, He is the Savior of your heart, your master, your God and
there is no other. Tell Him that you believe in the death,
burial, and resurrection of Christ as outlined in the books of
Matthew, Mark, Luke, and John.*

Know this, the victory belongs to Jesus Christ, stick with Him unto death. One more important note: No matter what do not ever *take a stamp, a chip, a mark of any type into your body (hand or forehead). It is the mark of the beast—666. Those who accept this mark pledge their allegiance to the Antichrist and Satan. They are going to hell and there is no going back.*

The peace of God and our Lord Jesus Christ be with you.

Joy

BETTER
DECEASED
THAN THE MARK
OF THE BEAST!

CHAPTER 11

Mr. 666

Higher and higher it went, to the delight of the largest live crowd ever assembled, until the helicopter itself seemed to fade. Now all they saw on the big screens were space and a large image taking shape. The fighter jets returned, but no one watched. They just listened and watched as the screen morphed into the image of a man wide as the heavens. Standing in midair among the planets in dramatic dark suit, white shirt, and power tie, feet spread, arms folded across his chest, teeth gleaming, eyes flashing and confident, was Nicolae Carpathia, gazing lovingly down on the faithful.

The image froze under Nicolae's benevolent gaze, and the roar from the crowd was deafening. All stood and wildly cheered and clapped and whistled . . .

The symbolism could not be lost on anyone. He may have been murdered. He may be dead. But Nicolae

Carpathia is alive in our hearts, and he is divine, and he is in Heaven watching over us.

—The Indwelling

LAMENTING LEADER'S LOSS

The slain great world leader lies in state. Thousands gather around his funeral bier while billions watch proceedings via satellite around the globe. As depicted in the *Left Behind* novel *The Indwelling,* the great leader will shortly show himself to be the beast of Revelation, chapter 13. His number, the familiar and mysterious 666, is destined to become a part of the mark of the beast system that will enslave most all people of Planet Earth.

Hollywood portrayed him as Damien Thorn in three films, *The Omen, Damien: Omen II,* and *Omen III: The Final Conflict,* a series that grossly strayed from the biblically prophetic story of Antichrist. For example, the movie version had Damien being the offspring of a union between Satan and a jackal. Public interest, however, was then, and continues to be, stimulated by this fascinating future tyrant.

ON BEST BEHAVIOR

The "man of sin," as he is called along with many other names in the Scriptures, will come on the scene as a great peacemaker, not as the devil incarnate. He will boast that he can do great things. He will personally guarantee peace between Israel and that nation's surrounding enemies.

ASTONISHING ACCOMPLISHMENT

As Yogi Berra once said: "It ain't bragging if you can do it." Antichrist will—at least for a short time—succeed in producing the peace no one has been able to bring about in the Middle East. That alone will make him seem a miracle worker.

Once again we look at the prophet Daniel's words about the world leader who will apparently solve the millennia-old Israeli-Arab conflict. "Then he shall confirm a covenant with many for one week; but in the middle of the week He shall bring an end to sacrifice and offering. And on the wing of abominations shall be one who makes desolate, even until the consummation, which is determined, is poured out on the desolate" (Daniel 9:27).

Many prophecy watchers believe that the present efforts to find the formula for peace in the Middle East will result in the seven-year covenant of the above Scriptures. When Antichrist guarantees Israel's peace and safety with this treaty, the Tribulation will begin.

Everything You Ever Wanted to Know about Antichrist, But Were Afraid to Ask

FIND IT FAST

There's much more prophesied to come from this man. He will give every appearance of arising from the dead after being wounded in the head (*Find It Fast:* Revelation 13:3). He and his religious leader/partner will perform great signs and wonders, miracles thought to be within God's abilities alone. He will claim to be Christ, while opposing Jesus Christ and God, the Father. People will be mesmerized by his rhetoric and his abilities. Ultimately, most will worship him. People will be forced to take a mark in their right hand or forehead as a sign of allegiance and worship. Those who refuse to do so will be killed by his regime.

UP CLOSE AND PERSONAL

Let's have, as they say, an up close and personal look at the prophesied world leader, who might even now be about to step upon the stage of end-time history. Bible prophecy doesn't give the exact year, day, or hour Antichrist will first appear. He will emerge from the world's sea of peoples, a leader that ultimately triumphs over all other outstanding politicians of the time. No one will recognize him as the final dictator.

RAPTURE-READY REALLY GOOD NEWS!

The best news for Christians is that while they might see his rise to world power, they won't ever know for certain this man's identity. That's because the Church must first be removed from Earth before the beast can be brought to full power—one more reason to be Rapture ready!

Paul the apostle writes of that in his 2 Thessalonians prophecies: "Let no one deceive you by any means; for that day [the Day of the Lord or the Tribulation period] will not come unless the falling away comes first, and the man of sin is revealed, the son of perdition . . . And now you know what is restraining, that he may be revealed in his own time. For the mystery of lawlessness is already at work; only He who now restrains will do so until He is taken out of the way" (2 Thessalonians 2:3, 6, 7).

KEEPING A LID ON EVIL

As described previously, the Church is the restraining influence on the world today, because God, the Holy Spirit, indwells each born-again believer. When the Church is raptured by Jesus, the Holy Spirit, who is omnipresent (always everywhere), will begin dealing again with mankind on Earth in the way He did before the Church came into existence at Pentecost (*Find It Fast:* Acts, chapter 2).

HAS ANTICHRIST ARRIVED?

The one who will be Antichrist could already be in the world. Prophetic signals of our time indicate that he probably is on the scene. But it is unlikely that Satan, much less the great man himself, knows his destiny for sure.

Paul prophesies that the whole world will know who he is, however, when the Church is removed. This man with a "wild beast" character will actually stand in the rebuilt Jewish temple atop Mount Moriah (the Temple Mount in Jerusalem), and declare himself to be God (*Find It Fast:* 2 Thessalonians 2:4). Then the persecution of Jews and Tribulation converts to Christianity will begin. It will be the bloodiest purge in human history, according to the words of Jesus himself: "For then there will be great tribulation, such as has not been since the beginning of the world until this time, no, nor ever shall be" (Matthew 24:21).

RAGING RELIGION

A religious leader will burst upon the world scene and gather the religions of the world into one great universal faith. That one-world religious system will then be invoked in the service of the Antichrist. Satanism will be the final form of worship that comes from this so-called church: "So they [the people of the world] worshipped the dragon [the devil] who gave authority to the beast; and they worshipped the beast, saying, 'Who is like the beast? Who is able to make war with him?' And he was given a mouth speaking great things and blasphemies . . ." (Revelation 13:4–5).

THE MALICIOUS MAESTRO

Satan himself is the master director of this all-inclusive, all-controlling religious system. The Bible describes in Revelation 13 the religious leader who will serve as Antichrist's false prophet.

REVELATION 13:11–14

The Antichrist will, shortly after establishing his power, be joined by an evil religious man termed the "false prophet." The second "beast," as the Bible calls him, will be able to perform acts that will appear to be supernatural. Because of his demonic power, the false prophet will fool most people of Earth into thinking they should worship the world leader as God. The religious man will call fire from the sky. He will probably have a part in supposedly causing the world leader, who is thought to be killed by a head wound, to come back to life. The false prophet will tell the people of Earth to make an image of the world leader. He will then force them to worship the image, which seems to miraculously move and speak.

PROFILING ANTICHRIST

The Bible gives many details about the Antichrist. This list, presented by the late Dr. Dave Breese, is as thorough as any we've found on the "Man of Sin." We recommend a careful study of the Scriptures given here, for those who want a better understanding of the coming beast of Revelation 13.

1. He will come presenting a great program of peace (Daniel 8:25).
2. He will oppose Christ (Daniel 8:25).
3. He will wear out the saints of God (Daniel 7:25).
4. He will come out of the area of the Old Roman Empire, which is present-day Europe (Daniel 9:26).
5. He will make a covenant with the nation of Israel (Daniel 9:27).
6. He will break that covenant and persecute the Jews (Daniel 9:27).
7. He will pretend to be God himself (2 Thessalonians 2:4).

8. He will occupy the rebuilt temple, the temple of God (2 Thessalonians 2:4).

9. He will perform the will of Satan (2 Thessalonians 2:9).

10. He will bring strong delusion to the whole world (2 Thessalonians 2:11).

11. He will be wounded to death, but he will recover (Revelation 13:14–15).

12. He will blaspheme God (Revelation 13:5–6).

13. All of the world will worship him (Revelation 13:8).

14. He will be a miracle worker (Revelation 13:13–14).

15. He will set up his image that speaks like a man (Revelation 13:14–15).

16. He will cause every person to receive a mark, the mark of the beast (Revelation 13:16).

17. He will himself have a number, 666 (Revelation 13:18).

Have You Seen This Man?

Ever since the Old Testament first spoke of him, Christians and Jews have been looking for the appearance of the Antichrist. Daniel described him as the most evil man who ever will live. He will charm the Jews into submission then turn against them. He will briefly become the most powerful man on Earth.

GUESSES GALORE

Many Christians have tried to select the Antichrist from among the men of their day. Some have made good assumptions, while others have been very much off base in their observations. Of course, none has been able to name the true Antichrist. Listed below are several world figures who have been tagged as being the Antichrist. Most of these men are dead and presumably off the hook, but a number of them are still active on the world stage.

⊕ **Antiochus Epiphanes** He was one of only a few pre-Christ figures considered as possible Antichrists, and he is described by scholars as being a type of Antichrist. Epiphanes was prophesied by Daniel the prophet (*Find It Fast:* Daniel 8:3–25), and he fulfilled many of the prophecies that the real Antichrist will repeat.

⊕ **Roman Emperor Nero** One of the first and one of the greatest persons to fit the role of Antichrist was Emperor Nero. He put many Christians to death, and even killed members of his own family. Nero's actions actually helped the Church to multiply faster. When he learned the Roman Senate was plotting against him, he died by poisoning himself.

⊕ **The Pope** Just about every pope has been accused of being the Antichrist. Antichrist will be a political beast, according to Revelation 13 and other prophetic passages. During the Middle Ages, when the political power of the pope was more pronounced, the pontiff's title was more plausible in considering who might be the Antichrist. Today, however, the political power of the pope has long since passed.

⊕ **Charlemagne** Charlemagne lived from A.D. 742–814 and controlled much of central Europe. Charlemagne put himself into the shoes of the Antichrist by trying to rebuild the Roman Empire. This is a task that only the real Antichrist will accomplish. Charlemagne died before achieving his goal.

⊕ **Napoleon** The self-crowned French emperor was not a particularly depraved man. He did not persecute the Church,

FIND
IT
FAST

and he lacked a number of the qualities needed for the role. His downfall was that he loved war too much. Napoleon, like Charlemagne, worked at reviving the Roman Empire. But, as we know, he didn't; rather, he met his Waterloo.

⊕ **Aleister Crowley** So evil that his nicknames were "the Beast" and "666," Aleister Crowley was a male witch who lived in England from 1875 to 1947. A number of rock and roll musicians, such as the Beatles, the Doors, and Ozzy Osbourne, featured references to him in or on their albums.

⊕ **Franklin Delano Roosevelt** The numerical value of FDR's name was reported to add up to 666. Because of the Great Depression, FDR was the most domineering U.S. president of the twentieth century. Roosevelt was in office for twelve years.

⊕ **Benito Mussolini** Because Mussolini became the dictator of Italy, the original capital of the Roman Empire, he was the subject of a great deal of commentary during his rule from 1922 to 1943. His extreme arrogance fit the role of Antichrist, but his military capabilities were laughable. Italy needed help from Germany all throughout World War II.

⊕ **Adolf Hitler** Most people would describe Hitler as the most villainous man who ever lived. He remains a demonic forewarning of what the real Antichrist will be like.

⊕ **Joseph Stalin** Russian dictator Joseph Stalin is believed to be the greatest mass murderer of all time, killing 30 million people. Most of history's tyrants killed foreigners; Stalin specialized in killing his own citizens. That in itself was enough to compel some to consider him a good candidate for Antichrist.

⊕ **Francisco Franco** Franco, the dictator of Spain from 1936 until his death in 1975, was called the Antichrist because of

his military control of the government of Spain and because
Nostradamus is said to have fingered him in one of his ram-
bling quatrains: "From Castille, Franco will bring out the as-
sembly. The ambassador will not agree and cause a schism:
The people of Rivera will be in the crowd, And they will refuse entry into the Gulf" (Century 9, Quatrain 16).

⊕ **John F. Kennedy** Many believed JFK, the nation's first
Roman Catholic president, would act together with the
pope to accomplish Catholic goals. These people believed a
future pope would be the false prophet, Antichrist's religious sidekick. At the 1956 Democratic convention,
Kennedy received 666 votes. When Kennedy was shot dead
in Dallas, several people waited for this deadly wound to
heal. It never happened.

⊕ **Henry Kissinger** Because of Secretary of State Kissinger's
activity in the Middle East, he was labeled by many as the
Antichrist. His raspy voice would be the first thing to dis-
qualify him, it would seem, since Antichrist will be a
speaker of unparalleled quality.

⊕ **King Juan Carlos of Spain** The late prophecy teacher
Charles Taylor was a big proponent of the idea of Carlos
being the Antichrist because of his bloodline and because
he's the king of the eleventh nation to join the European
Union.

⊕ **Ayatollah Khomeini** Khomeini, one of the grumpiest men
to ever live, termed America the "great Satan" and bedeviled
the U.S. for a number of years.

⊕ **Ronald Wilson Reagan** Say it isn't so, Ron. During the
1980s when Reagan was president of the U.S., there was
talk going around about the fact that he had six letters in

each of his three names. Also, there was a buzz going around about the numbers in the address of his California home that gave Antichrist hunters the heebie jeebies.

⊕ **Mikhail Gorbachev** Gorbachev, the first Russian leader to supposedly support the rights of the people, has been and still remains a candidate for the job of Antichrist. Until Gorby dies, prophecy watchers will have an eye on him. Apparently, being born with that mark on his head was too obvious for some.

⊕ **Saddam Hussein** Even before the Gulf War, Saddam was looked on as the "beast" prophesied in Daniel and Revelation. During and after that conflict, he gained a dominant footing as a leading candidate for the job.

⊕ **Maitreya** A camera-shy New Age personage who is said to be on this Earth somewhere is waiting for his opportunity to save the world. It is our judgment that Maitreya is more myth than man.

⊕ **Sun Myung Moon** The leader of the Unification Church openly claims to be the Messiah. Moon recently was sent to jail for tax evasion. Jesus, by having a tax collector on his staff, didn't suffer from tax problems. You pick which one was the smarter messiah.

⊕ **Yasser Arafat** When Palestinian Liberation Organization (PLO) leader Arafat signed the peace treaty with Israel in 1993, some thought that he was bringing to pass the prophecy regarding the Antichrist signing a seven-year peace treaty with Israel. In order for this to be the case, we would have to be well into the Tribulation Period.

⊕ **Louis Farrakhan** Farrakhan has worked hard to earn the title of Antichrist: He has met with every Islamic dictator

there is, and he's called the Jewish faith "a gutter religion."
Farrakhan has said that Jesus was "just a prophet" and that
he, Louis Farrakhan, is the true Jesus.

⊕ **Karl Hapsburg** Just like Juan Carlos, Karl Hapsburg has a
good shot at becoming the Antichrist—at least on paper—
simply because of who he is. His family holds the title of
ruler over Jerusalem. The Hapsburg family also reigned
over the Holy Roman Empire at one time. The European
Union will be a revival of the Roman Empire.

⊕ **William Jefferson Clinton** A number of folks have e-mailed
Todd Strandberg saying, "Clinton is Satan's pet." Todd
came across information posted in newsgroups and Web
sites that, through a complicated series of mathematical
gymnastics, equate William Jefferson Clinton's name with
the beastly number 666.

⊕ **Sam Donaldson** So many people submitted ABC newsman
Donaldson's name for the designation of Antichrist that he
was finally added to this list. By including Sam, we hope we
don't cause any jealousy at the other networks.

⊕ **Barney the Dinosaur** Because John, the writer of Revelation,
would have never known what a dinosaur looked like, it's logical to assume he would have identified any vision of Barney
as being a dragon. Taking this into consideration, you might
find the following Scriptures quite revealing: "And another
sign appeared in heaven: behold, a great, fiery red dragon . . ."
(Revelation 12:3); "So they worshiped the dragon who gave
authority to the beast; and they worshiped the beast, saying,
'Who is like the beast? Who is able to make war with him?' "
(Revelation 13:4); and "He laid hold of the dragon, that ser-
pent of old, who is the Devil and Satan, and bound him for a
thousand years" (Revelation 20:2).

⊕ **Bill Gates** If the beast needs to be computer literate and financially well off, then founder and CEO of Microsoft Bill Gates would be a good candidate. It is common knowledge that Gates is strictly a computer nerd, so it's hard to imagine him evolving into a skillful political leader.

⊕ **Prince Charles of Wales** We are told that Prince Charles could be the beast. Charles has the familiar numerology claims made about him—claims that the numerology behind his name equals 666. He is believed to have ancestral links to the Roman Empire. It was also reported that he had identifier chips implanted in his young sons for quick location in case of kidnapping. He's got a head start on the "mark of the beast" prophetic scenario.

⊕ **Jacques Chirac** French President Jacques Chirac has been involved in a flurry of diplomatic activity. His high profile has caught the attention of several prophecy watchers.

ADDITIONAL ANALYSIS ABOUT ANTICHRIST

Here are some observations about the Antichrist. We have no idea who the Antichrist is. When one examines history, it becomes evident that people who become well known on the world stage were often largely unknowns before they became famous. Hitler is a good example. Before he ruled much of Europe, at one low point, he was living in a flophouse. If you had walked by and seen him, you would have never guessed he would someday threaten to take over the world.

Prophecy scholars who study this future leader's profile in the Bible have concluded that Satan has most likely had a man ready to fulfill that prophetic role at any given time in history. Satan knows

God doesn't lie. God has said there will arise a leader who will be totally evil. John the prophet calls him Antichrist.

Satan, however, is not all knowing. He doesn't know who the man of sin will be any more than we do. He just knows that he will arise. Some believe that Satan grooms a special man, such as Adolf Hitler, or someone else, during every appropriate period of history. So far, none has been that last world dictator.

When the time for the Antichrist comes, he will achieve great power, but right now he could be out pumping gas at some service station.

DON'T SELL HIM SHORT

The word "Antichrist" has lost much of its meaning in recent years. To call someone "Antichrist" in the past was on the same level as cursing. Now, thanks in large part to Hollywood and its fictional misrepresentations, attaching the name to someone or something brings up mythological connections. The same thing applies to calling someone a devil. Using familiar or recognizable names to try to identify the one who will be Antichrist, for example Barney the Dinosaur or Bill Gates, only helps blur the real significance of the character termed Antichrist. Someday he will rise to power and cause the destruction of more human beings than anyone who has ever lived. There has never been a person so evil or so powerful.

MR. 666 GETS WHAT'S COMING TO HIM

How will Antichrist meet his end? The prophetic Scripture foretells that when Christ comes again in brilliant glory, He will destroy Antichrist's armies with the power of His voice. This will happen at the end of the war called Armageddon.

When Christ comes again with great power and glory, the Bible says, He will defeat the Antichrist, whom He will then, along with the false prophet, order to be thrown into the lake that burns with fire and brimstone forever and ever. It is wise to consider the lesson of Antichrist's fate. The lesson of his tragic end is that evil will not finally triumph. Like Lucifer and the rebellion he led against God before the world was created, all who attempt to take God's throne from him suffer insanity. It just won't happen!

ANTICHRIST SPIRIT

The Antichrist spirit written about by John the apostle in 1 John 4:3 is alive and well today. Humanists have tried to do things their own way since the time of the Tower of

FIND IT FAST

Babel (*Find It Fast*: Genesis, chapter 11) and even before. Man still attempts to push God off the planet. They want no one and nothing to rule over them. Antichrist will be the ultimate product of man's foolish try at becoming gods.

The Antichrist will appear at first to succeed at all he attempts. He will be largely successful in gathering the wealth of the world into his treasuries. That wealth will be—as it is by dictators of our time—distributed to the elite who can help him accomplish his earth-enslaving goals. Soon after assuming full power, however, he will turn on even his most ardent supporters and assert his own prideful will.

Phenomenal Failure

But he will soon meet his doom in total defeat and eternal destruction. The following are some further thoughts from Dr. Breese about the downfall of Antichrist and, at the same time, the rewards of God's saints:

1. He and his power will be destroyed by the brightness of the coming of Jesus Christ (2 Thessalonians 2:8).
2. The saints of God will share in the final defeat of the Antichrist when Jesus comes again (Revelation 19:14).
3. The Antichrist and the false prophet, his religious associate, who wrought miracles and deceived the world, will be cast alive into a lake of fire burning with brimstone (Revelation 19:20).
4. He is found in that lake of fire a thousand years later, and there the beast and the false prophet will be tormented day and night forever and ever (Revelation 20:10). ("Europe

and the Prince That Shall Come," a chapter by Dave Breese in *Storming Toward Armageddon: Essays in Apocalypse* by William Terry James. Green Forest, Arkansas: New Leaf Press, 1992).

END-TIME AILMENTS AND RAPTURE-READY RX

Antichristophobia Condition that causes sufferers to declare almost every world leader to be the Antichrist. They will focus on a single personality to the point of neglecting more significant end-time events.

Symptoms These people refuse to vote in any general election because they don't want to stand accused of electing the Antichrist to office. They only watch leaders who are prominent on the world stage.

Treatment Should bear in mind that the Antichrist will not come to power until after the Rapture: "Then he shall confirm a covenant with many for one week; but in the middle of the week He shall bring an end to sacrifice and offering. And on the wing of abominations shall be one who makes desolate, even until the consummation, which is determined, is poured out on the desolate."

IF THE BEAST'S
NOT ENOUGH
THERE'S MORE
SCARY STUFF!

CHAPTER 12

Scary, Scary Stuff

David guessed the temperature at 110 degrees. He couldn't remember being out at mid-day in New Babylon when it was this hot . . . There was no wind. Just the relentless sun, the body heat of four million people, and the acrid smoke from the imposing statue.

The image began to move, as if an earth tremor made it sway and bounce, but nothing else was affected. All eyes turned toward it in terror and word spread quickly throughout the courtyard that something was happening. For a long minute the thing seemed to vibrate in place. Then it rocked, and the smoke began to billow once more.

The image soon glowed red hot, and the smoke poured out so fast that it again formed clouds that darkened the sky. The temperature dropped immediately, but going from daylight to dusk so quickly made many fall to their faces.

—The Indwelling

PLANETARY PUNISHMENT

FIND IT FAST

People of the Tribulation era gather at New Babylon for the funeral of the much-beloved world leader who was assassinated. The novel *The Indwelling* depicts a mourning throng of people who are about to see fulfillment of prophecy found in Revelation, chapter 13.

The disappearance of millions is a fading memory, as the changed world order is now approximately three and one-half years into post-Rapture history. Little do the 4 million people gathered at the world headquarters called New Babylon realize they are about to enter an era more fearful by far than any other.

JUMP-STARTED JUDGMENTS

God's judgments will begin to unfold in a stepped-up way from this point forward. The supposedly resurrected world leader will soon begin his reign of unprecedented atrocities upon the Jewish race, and all who have genuinely converted to Christianity.

Antichrist's Cronies

Even his followers are in for horrific experiences, because the Antichrist will abide nothing and no one who is not totally devoted to him. The slightest hint of disloyalty will bring his regime's wrath. Antichrist is now indwelt by Satan, himself, and Lucifer, the fallen one, has been confined to Earth. His anger is supernatural, as is his strength. It will literally be a time of hell on Earth. All who haven't accepted Jesus Christ, and who go into that era, are scheduled to endure some scary, scary things.

God Outpunishes the Devil

God's punishments will be worse for the rebels on Planet Earth than will Satan's wrath against God's saints, and against God's chosen people, the Jewish race. God will deal judgments upon all who oppose his will in a series of three periods. Each period will contain seven specific judgments each, for a total of twenty-one. As when the Lord judged the Egyptian pharaoh during the time of the Israelites' exodus, each judgment will get progressively worse. These judgments will lead to the time at the end of Armageddon, when Jesus Christ will return from Heaven in glory and power.

Unmatched Violence

Before Christ's return to make all things on Earth right again, there will come the most violent times that have ever been. This is not something most folks care to think too long and hard about.

KILL THE MESSENGER!

"Why are you trying to scare people?" Often such messages come in from people who are irate over what they see as fear mongering. Of course, that question has always been puzzling. The tendency is to think that their negative reaction is based on a rebellious rejection of the truth.

Truth Troubling

A number of people express that Bible prophecy repulses them. They make it quite clear that they are genuinely bothered by the idea of the prophetic truth, which they instinctively seem to know will someday invade their personal worlds. With no intention of implying these folks are on the same par with demons, it must be said that even the demonic angels that encountered Jesus were troubled by the knowledge that their time of freedom was limited: "And suddenly they cried out, saying, 'What have we to do with You, Jesus, You Son of God? Have You come here to torment us before the time?' " (Matthew 8:29).

Those doomed beings, who followed Lucifer in his rebellion before the world as we know it was created, don't want to face up to their end, which they know is as sure for them as the next tick of the clock. It's not just that they don't want their good times tormenting people interrupted; they don't want to be reminded of what prophecy says is their ultimate end.

God, Not Us, in Charge

It is understandable that some people are hostile to the truth, but still, it shouldn't matter what any prophecy writer or speaker says or believes. The Tribulation hour doesn't need our approval or help. God is the only one controlling the eternal schedule: "And [the Lord] said to them, 'It is not for you to know times or seasons which the Father has put in His own authority' " (Acts 1:7).

THE FUTURE IS SCARY

A lot of scholars try to apologize for the horrors detailed by prophecy. After frequently being labeled "prophets of doom," many end-time teachers now make a habit of saying the world is not actually going to end. It's true that the Bible does say Planet Earth will still be here at the conclusion of the seven-year Tribulation . . . but it doesn't give mankind any guarantees.

Doomsday Destined

Those who work to draw the world's attention to prophecy are indeed announcers of doom. Any way you cut it, you can't get away from the fact. The Bible repeatedly warns of an approaching time of unimaginable wrath, so like it or not, doom is coming our way.

During the Tribulation, famine, natural disasters, war, and disease will create the worst time of suffering in all of human history. Again, we read the warning by Jesus:

"For then there will be great tribulation, such as has not been since the beginning of the world until this time, no, nor ever shall be" (Matthew 24:21).

The Bible doesn't say exactly what percentage of the world's population will perish, but it's clear that the death rate will be very high. If you add up the judgments of Revelation, it would seem to indicate at least two-thirds will be wiped out. Jesus said if He didn't return at the end of the Tribulation to put an end to the fighting, every living thing that has flesh would die (*Find It Fast:* Mark 13:20).

There is one simple reason why the Tribulation is going to be so

FIND
IT
FAST

terrible: God will be trying His best to get man's attention. Every time God judges the Earth, the observation is made that man refused to repent for his evil deeds.

Salvation Survives

Some folks believe that most people left behind after the Rapture will be barred from finding salvation. A quick check of the Bible, however, proves that God's invitation to repent is offered without any limitations. For example, we read in Revelation 9:20–21: "But the rest of mankind, who were not killed by these plagues, did not repent of the works of their hands, that they should not worship demons, and idols of gold, silver, brass, stone, and wood, which can neither see nor hear nor walk. And they did not repent of their murders or their sorceries or their sexual immorality or their thefts."

Devil Deceives but Christ Calls

Because deception will abound, most people will not respond to the warnings. Despite the devil doing his best to deceive man, however, some people will see the light and give their lives to Christ. The prophet John wrote that the number of people saved out of the Tribulation will be so large that no man will be able to number their ranks (*Find It Fast:* Revelation 7:9, 14).

Life-and-Death Choice

Anyone considering becoming a believer once the Rapture has taken place will have to make a tough choice between life and death. He or she will have the option of either submitting to the Antichrist's rule or facing martyrdom. Those who decide to follow the Antichrist will be compelled to receive a mark that will leave them eternally damned.

Taking the martyrdom route is no picnic. It is true that many believers will survive to the end of the Tribulation, but these will be few in comparison to the ones who must give their lives.

Mercy through Darkness

We should never try to take away from the magnitude of how dismal it will be for those people who find themselves trapped in the Tribulation period. Yet, even in Earth's darkest time, God's mercy will still be found. In most cases, mercy will not come in the form of deliverance. It will be evident in the saints' ability to withstand the trials facing them.

Wishcraft for the Wicked

It's amazing how many people believe that you can wish something into being. The strength of a person's optimism does not govern reality. It doesn't matter how much you believe you're going to win some big national sweepstakes, your chances are still around 100 million to one.

One of the most shocking examples of how dangerous overly

positive thinking can be was presented on a TV program. A newscast showed some teenagers trying to videotape one of them jumping over a speeding car. The kids were reported to be reenacting a TV program that featured a guy doing similar moronic things, such as diving into septic tanks and lighting himself on fire.

Each of the four boys involved in this stunt was age seventeen or younger. All of them were obviously lacking intelligence, but one sixteen-year-old was clearly the most brain dead. While one of the boys held a video camera on the roadside to record this fiasco, two of them raced toward their buddy at a high rate of speed. When the car reached our foolhardy hero, he tried to jump over the car, but he didn't quite make it. He managed to get as high as the windshield of the car. Instantly, he shattered the windshield, crumpled the hood of the car, and broke as many bones in his body as did Evel Knievel during a lifetime of daredevil jumps.

Needing a Reality Check

What could have caused these young jokers to defy so many God-given rules of common sense? The answer is that they had their own view of reality. Their blind optimism certainly had zero influence over the laws of physics. The boy who was severely injured will now have physical scars with him the rest of his life to remind him of the need for good judgment.

People who try to shun the reality of the end times are in for an equally dreadful surprise. Simply slapping a happy face on world events doesn't work. The power of positive thinking cannot mitigate the fact that the truth is the truth and a lie is a lie.

NO MORE MR. NICE GOD

From day one, mankind has been entangled in a multitude of errors regarding the characteristics of God. A large portion of the population has refused to believe in a divine being. Of those people who do believe in a great "I Am," many have a grievous misunderstanding of God's disdain for acts of disobedience.

Supreme Standards

We've met people who basically believe the Lord has no standards regarding sin. The average person you'd meet on the street will tell you, "Well, I've been a pretty good person most of my life."

Anyone working on a military post must show an ID card or have a military sticker on his or her car in order to enter the post. Those lacking the proper authority are turned away at the gate. Heaven will also have requirements for all people seeking to enter its gates.

Gentle Jesus Not Judgmental

The humble image of Jesus riding into Jerusalem on a donkey, or sitting on a rock talking with children, seems to be permanently implanted in people's minds. There's another image of Jesus, however, with which those who have only that picture of Him need to become familiar. It's a Jesus who is holding a rod of iron and dispensing judgment on the nations. The Bible is full of ominous comments about God's sternness. For example: "And the kings of the earth, the great men, the rich men, the commanders, the mighty men, every slave and every free man, hid themselves in the caves and in the rocks of the mountains, and said to the mountains and rocks, 'Fall on us and hide us from the face of Him who sits on the throne and from the wrath of the Lamb! For the great day of His wrath has come, and who is able to stand?'" (Revelation 6:15–17).

Reason for Reporting Wrath

One of the main reasons we continue to maintain the prophecy Web sites, write the prophecy books, and speak on prophecy topics is that someday we are going to have to go before the Lord of Lords and give an account of our lives. No doubt many of us have read some of the lighter references that show God's merciful side; however, there are also some rather strong words to describe how strictly our earthly deeds will be judged:

⊕ "Knowing, therefore, the terror of the Lord, we persuade men . . ." (2 Corinthians 5:11).
⊕ "If the righteous one is scarcely saved, where will the ungodly and the sinner appear?" (1 Peter 4:18).

THE GREAT ESCAPE

Nonbelievers, and sadly, even some believers, love to complain about how prophetic-minded Christians are fascinated with dire circumstances. It is true that if you look at the daily news page on any of the main prophecy sites, you'll find probably around 90 percent of the posted news articles deal with every type of calamity under the sun.

It is true also, that, as said before, we are often accused of trying to scare people. It seems odd, then, that, even though we're heavily criticized for trying to scare people, we are rarely asked why we're so eager to post bad news.

If we were asked that question, the answer would be that bad news is what seems to draw people, even the critics of prophecy teaching. There is a side to man that loves to wallow in negativity.

But our motivations are all positive. We emphasize the coming terrors because God has commanded that people be warned. And the mercy and love and grace of God are most starkly displayed when contrasted against the darkness of Tribulation judgments.

Prophecy and Priorities

Our interest in prophecy has largely been based on the realization that the Rapture event will someday overshadow in importance all things earthly. A person—one who is Rapture ready—might have plans to get married next week or enter a pie-eating contest. However, if the Rapture comes today, those plans become insignificant. As a matter of fact, they become null and void. Prophecy can focus the Christian's mind on what God sees as life's true priorities.

Profiling Pre-Trib Opponents

Before the Tribulation begins, all believers are going to be supernaturally caught up to Heaven. This is the "blessed hope, and the glorious appearing of the great God and our Savior Jesus Christ" that the Apostle Paul spoke of in Titus 2:13.

We are constantly being dogged by Post-Trib folks who abhor the idea of a Pre-Tribulation Rapture. Because it doesn't involve us suffering for our faith, the Rapture is something they can't accept.

Guidelines for God?

It could be argued: What business do they have telling God how to conduct His affairs? Why do they insist that He insists that Christians have to go through the Tribulation? Are they correct when they contend that God sends those who have accepted His Son through that horrendous time so they can do enough good deeds to make them more righteous? Must Christians prove their salvation as genuine by being martyred or by "enduring" to the end—something God has not foreordained for Christians of the Church Age?

Hanging On for Dear Life?!

If Christians must work as hard as they can in order to be saved, what does this say about Jesus having shed His blood to save the lost? The Bible says He did it all on the cruel cross at Calvary. Do Christians have to help Him out in saving their eternal souls?

If Christians must go through the Tribulation, why must not all the Christians who have lived since the cross also have to go through that era of terror to prove themselves as well?

A Martyrdom Mystery

True, many bled and died during times of great martyrdom, and thus might qualify for such self-help in the salvation of their own souls. But what about twentieth-century Americans who were Christians but who have died? Does the fact they can't go through the Tribulation mean they are now unsaved? Certainly, few of them died for their faith.

Maybe they all must now be resurrected from death, just so they can go through the time of Antichrist in order to prove what big, brave Christians they are.

THE GOOD NEWS

These things are, of course, ludicrous. Christ paid the price once and for all, for those who will but trust Him to save their eternal souls. There is nothing anyone can do but believe in this grace process. That's why the Gospel is called the "Good News."

"Rapture Ready" Requirements

However, we do partly agree that a price must be paid. Actually, a profoundly genuine decision must be made, to put it more correctly. To qualify for the Rapture, you have to be a believer. A large portion of the population will greatly regret missing the Rapture.

If it was made known that the translation of the Church was going to take place tomorrow, you could expect everyone to be on his or her knees tonight confessing sins. After the Rapture, one of the greatest shockers is likely going to be how many people didn't truly know Christ as Savior. Whether a person has genuinely accepted Christ for salvation is a matter only between the person and God, so far as the eternal disposition of his or her soul is concerned.

Jesus said about being ready for the Rapture: "Watch ye therefore, and pray always, that ye may be accounted worthy to escape all these things that shall come to pass, and to stand before the Son of man" (Luke 21:36). To be watching for Christ's coming in the Rapture is something that Jesus not only recommended, but commanded.

Jesus' words contain much more than the directive to simply watch for His sudden appearance. He told the Christian to pray always. In so doing, He implied, one will be found worthy to escape all these things that are coming upon the Earth.

Praying always, in the sense Jesus used it here, means that the person is constantly desiring to be in sync with the Lord. He or she is walking with Christ. Jesus' prayer to His Father in Heaven in John, chapter 17, gives the complete story of this union and what it means to Him, to the believer, and to God the Father.

Worthiness, Not Worthlessness

FIND
IT
FAST

To be "worthy," to escape all the things that are to come, is to be doing what the Bible directs the Christian to do. In other words, living the Christian life in the biblically pre-scribed way. Again, however, it is Christ, not the believer, who keeps the believer from eternal damnation, and from the hour of Tribulation (*Find It Fast:* Revelation 3:10). But the Christian who wants to hear his Lord say, "Well done, my good and faithful servant . . ." (Matthew 25:23) will always strive to walk the Christian walk as well as talk the talk.

ESCAPE WHAT THINGS?

The Christian, then, is to always try to prove himself or herself wor-thy to escape "all these things," and to "stand before the Son of man." What are "all these things," and what does it mean "to stand before the Son of man"?

All These Things

There are some things that Jesus indicated are well worth escaping. These constitute the "Scary, Scary Stuff" of this chapter's title. We have looked at some of the things of the Tribulation era that are prophesied to occur. We will continue to deal with these frightening matters in the balance of the book. But this might be a good place to put them in a nutshell for quick review.

Following the Rapture of Christ's Church (all born-again believers who are alive at the time it occurs), prophesied things will start popping quickly.

- ⊕ Total chaos will rule for a time.
- ⊕ Governments will get control through sometimes harsh methods.
- ⊕ A one-world government will come together.
- ⊕ A one-world church will form.
- ⊕ A world leader from Europe will step to the forefront and take charge of the peace process.
- ⊕ The Israeli government and Israel's enemies will sign an agreement of peace that ensures peace and safety.
- ⊕ Peace will not last, as a coalition of nations, led by Russia, will invade the Middle East.
- ⊕ God, himself, will destroy all but one-sixth of the invader forces.
- ⊕ Much of the world will be hit by the deadly effects of the invasion. This will possibly include chemical, biological, and nuclear aftereffects.
- ⊕ The world leader will solidify his power following the Russian-led coalition's destruction.

⊕ Two Old Testament–type prophets will come onto the world scene and preach about Christ, while condemning the world's evil.

⊕ Meanwhile, God will put His protection upon 144,000 Jews who have converted to Christianity, so that they can begin to preach God's saving message to the people of the Tribulation.

⊕ At the same time, God will allow strong delusion to come over all who heard the Gospel before the Rapture but, fully understanding the offer of salvation, refused to accept Christ. These will believe Antichrist's, and Satan's, lies.

⊕ Antichrist, after months of trying, will finally murder the two Old Testament–type prophets. But they will come back to life and be taken into Heaven while the world watches.

⊕ Antichrist will receive a supposedly deadly head wound.

⊕ He will appear to resurrect from the dead, being now possessed by Satan.

⊕ Antichrist will stand in the Temple on Mount Moriah in Jerusalem. He will claim to be God, and demand worship.

⊕ The false prophet will direct all worship to Antichrist, and will erect an image of him.

⊕ Antichrist's regime will institute a computer mark and numbers system. It will be both to control the world's populations and to cause all to worship Antichrist, whose number in all of this is 666.

⊕ Those who refuse to accept Antichrist's mark will be murdered. Beheading will apparently be the regime's chosen method of offing these "traitors."

⊕ Antichrist will begin a systematic genocide against the Jewish race that will make Hitler's holocaust look mild by comparison.

⊕ He and the false prophet will also have all the new believers they can find rounded up, tortured, and then murdered.

⊕ While Antichrist hunts down and murders people by the millions, God's judgments will begin to fall directly on the rebellious people of Planet Earth.

⊕ Millions upon millions will die while God's wrath pours out in a series of three types of judgments, each consisting of seven specific judgments, for a total of twenty-one judgments.

⊕ When all is said and done, more than one-half, possibly as much as two-thirds, of all human life on Earth will die of the plagues.

⊕ God will prepare, and the Jewish remnant will flee to, a hiding place, probably Petra, the ancient city carved in the rose red–colored rocks of the Jordanian wilderness.

⊕ Antichrist and his forces, led by Satan, will pursue the Jewish people and try to murder them, but the pursuing forces will be swallowed up by the Earth.

⊕ While the Jewish and many of the Gentile people still alive remain safely protected, God's wrath will fall in greater force.

⊕ The sun will go partly dark, while at the same time heating up to seven times hotter than normal.

⊕ A great object will fall into the ocean from space. Its impact will kill life in the sea, and most likely will destroy coastal areas with tidal waves.

⊕ Another asteroid or other mass from space will strike Earth and will poison much of the planet's freshwater sources.

⊕ Great, unprecedented earthquakes will happen simultaneously all over the Earth.

⊕ People will be so frightened they will have heart attacks, just from the things they see are yet to come.

⊕ A supernatural plague of huge insectlike creatures will be released from the abyss, and they will sting all who have the mark of the beast. Men and women will try to commit suicide because of their great pain from the stings and bites of these demonic creatures.

⊕ God will then move in the minds of all military forces on Earth to gather in the valley of Jezreel, the plains of Esdraelon, near the ancient city of Megiddo. This is Armageddon.

⊕ The "Kings of the East," a huge army out of the Orient numbering more than 200 million troops, will invade to make war with Antichrist's and the other world forces.

⊕ Jesus said of this time that if He didn't come back, everyone and everything would die because of the fighting about to take place.

⊕ Jesus will return with the armies of Heaven. His armies consist of the mighty angels and Jesus' Church, which was raptured at least seven years earlier.

⊕ Antichrist's armies and all others will try to prevent Christ's return.

⊕ Jesus will simply speak, and all armies on Earth will be rendered helpless, most killed.

Scary, scary stuff, huh? But it will all happen. You have God's Word, not ours, on that. A bunch of good reasons to be "Rapture ready," and to be found worthy to stand before Jesus, don't you think?

END-TIME AILMENTS AND RAPTURE-READY RX

Tribulation Mania This is a delusional state of mind that causes people to look forward to the Tribulation. This condition most frequently strikes people who believe Jesus is coming for the Church after the Tribulation.

Symptoms These people are verbally committed to going through the Tribulation. They typically have no established game plan for how they will survive the seven years of hell on Earth.

Treatment A strong dose of reality is highly recommended. The Tribulation will most likely require that most believers be martyred for their faith. "And I saw thrones, and they sat on them, and judgment was committed to them. Then I saw the souls of those who had been beheaded for their witness to Jesus and for the word of God, who had not worshiped the beast or his image, and had not received his mark on their foreheads or on their hands. And they lived and reigned with Christ for a thousand years" (Revelation 20:4).

REPENT OF
SINS OR
SATAN WINS!

CHAPTER 13

When the Almighty's Salesmen Come Calling

CNN was broadcasting live from Jerusalem, where two men had tried to attack the preachers at the Wailing Wall. Dan Bennett was on the scene for CNN.

"It was an ugly and dangerous confrontation for what many here are calling the two heretical prophets, known only as Moishe and Eli," Bennett said. "We know these names only because they have referred to each other thus, but we have been unable to locate anyone who knows any more about them . . . They have been taking turns speaking—preaching, if you will—for hours and continuing to claim that Jesus Christ is the Messiah. They have proclaimed over and over that the great worldwide disappearances last week, including many here in Israel, evidenced Christ's rapture of his church . . ."

—*Left Behind*

PROBLEM PREACHERS

Two strange men, dressed in ancient prophet's garb, stand together in the streets of Jerusalem. They preach loudly, proclaiming that Jesus Christ is Israel's true Messiah. They tell that these are the times prophesied in the ancient foretellings of the Bible.

The people of Jerusalem surround them, listening to what they say, but they quickly turn against them because of their message. Soldiers try to attack them but fall dead at their feet, untouched by the prophets themselves.

This prophecy is foretold in Revelation 11:3: "And I will give power to my two witnesses, and they will prophesy one thousand two hundred and sixty days, clothed in sackcloth."

Man Rules

The novel *Left Behind* pictures a crowd of onlookers who are decidedly in favor of the heavily armed military force, rather than on the side of the preachers. It is a time when the new world order is well underway in the post-Rapture era. People have, for the most part, bought into the humanist lie that man, not God, has the answers to their growing dilemmas.

These two crazy religious fanatics are trying to disrupt the promised peace by preaching a bigoted message that Jesus, a troublemaker crucified long ago in this very city, is the only way to salvation.

Deadly Deception

Things are scheduled to get much, much darker for the world from here, although the false promises will paint a bright picture for the future. The deception will grow stronger while Antichrist's power increases and Satan more and more has his way with the inhabitants of Planet Earth.

Most people will not want to hear anything but words that promise to return things to the way they were before all the chaos, confusion, and economic downturn took place following the disappearance disaster.

The world leader, who by this time will have emerged to the top of world politics, tells them what they want to hear. They will be more eager to hang onto his every word than were those of the Great Depression era eager to hold on to the promises of Franklin D. Roosevelt.

False Faith Followers

While the people of Earth don't want to hear the message of Christ, and salvation, they will soon, according to Bible prophecy, embrace the emerging one-world religious message of peace and unity. They will believe that man is, in the final analysis, the only hope for bringing an ideal existence upon the planet. The false religious system, with the prophesied false prophet leading the way, will nourish the notion that man is his own god, that each human is, himself or herself, a god, or part of the universal godhood.

GOD'S CHOSEN CHUMPS

Israel, in particular, will put its collective faith in the world leader, who will assure their peace and safety. The prophecy concerning this peace covenant, again, is found in the first part of Daniel 9:27: "Then he shall confirm a covenant with many for one week . . ."

The Jews will embrace the Antichrist, even though they, as a race and a religious people, cried "Crucify Him!" when Jesus offered himself as their Messiah. That action of embracing the world leader as a sort of messiah that can save them from their enemies will cause God's righteous jealousy and anger to rise to full fury.

God Chastises His Chosen

The Jewish race is God's chosen people, and He will not abide them being unfaithful to Him. Thus will begin the Tribulation, during which God will purge out of Israel a few people who will choose to love and obey Him.

The second part of the Daniel 9:27 prophecy states that after the guarantee of peace and security for Israel will come Antichrist's complete betrayal against Israel, and deadly persecution by his regime: "But in the middle of the week He shall bring an end to sacrifice and offering. And on the wing of abominations shall be one who makes desolate, even until the consummation, which is determined, is poured out on the desolate" (Daniel 9:27).

Beast Breaks Bargain

Antichrist, after confirming a seven-year peace treaty between Israel and her enemies, will allow the Jews to rebuild their temple on the Temple Mount in Jerusalem. They will reinstitute animal sacrifice—a practice that was ended when the Jewish temple was destroyed in A.D. 70. But halfway into the Tribulation (as well as halfway into the peace covenant), the beast of Revelation 13 will enter the temple, make the Jews stop worshipping there, and proclaim himself to be God (*Find It Fast:* 2 Thessalonians 2:4).

Remnant Rescued

The people who make it through the terrible years of murderous persecution by Antichrist will go into the thousand-year reign of Jesus Christ. This is known as the Millennium. These Jewish people, along with the Gentile people who make it through alive, will repopulate the Earth. The Jews, who are the remnant, will form the promised nation of Israel, where Jesus will be king, and sit upon the prophesied throne of David.

THE MIRACLE NATION

God is perfectly righteous and fair in every sense. First of all, **He always keeps His promises.** For example, He promised that Israel would again become a nation after being dispersed all over the world. No other nation has been completely done away with as a nation, then scattered for thousands of years, then regathered with their native language again becoming part of their national life. But that is exactly what happened to Israel, just as God promised.

God even prophesied that Israel would be reborn in a single day: "Who has heard such a thing? Who has seen such things? Shall the earth be made to give birth in one day? Or shall a nation be born at once?" (Isaiah 66:8). This prophecy was fulfilled when modern Israel was miraculously reborn on May 14, 1948—in a single day! "Miraculous" is the proper word, because that nation came to life in the midst of a war raging all about. Millions opposed her birth, but God had other ideas. He had foretold the event through Isaiah the prophet thousands of years before the nation's modern birth!

God Doesn't Give Up

Secondly, **God has never given up on man.** Even with the flood of Noah's day, when the world had become totally corrupted, the Lord saved Noah and his seven family members to repopulate the planet. In His perfect righteousness and fairness, He will not give up on man even during the upcoming Tribulation, when the whole world will seemingly reject His every effort to lovingly bring them back into His family—even to the point of offering His only Son, Jesus, as the sacrificial Lamb that takes away the sins of the world.

Countering the Counterfeit

While Antichrist and his false prophet, under Satan's direction, deceives the world with their lie that man is his own god, the true God of Heaven will send a powerful counter to the devilish attempt to keep all of mankind lost, apart from God, their Creator.

God's counter to Satan's evangelism of lies involves two particular sets of preachers who will proclaim the saving message of Jesus Christ. The first set of salesmen, we've already looked at to some extent. They are the two witnesses. The second set is made up of thousands.

SALVATION SUPER SALESMEN

They will have to be super salesmen, that's for sure. Their job will be tougher than, as they say, selling ice to Eskimos. But these folks will have supernatural gifts and talents to apply to their seemingly impossible sales job. And, God, the Holy Spirit, will be with them on every sales call.

Starting from Ground Zero

When the Rapture occurs, everyone on the planet will be on equal ground. That is, no one will be Christian. Many will still claim Christianity as their theological base after the Rapture. These will not have been "born again" by believing in Christ and what He did on the cross for their salvation. These will claim that living a good life, doing good to others, giving money to worthy causes, being kind to strangers, caring for animals, and even protecting the forests form the basis for their being Christians.

They will have been left behind in the great disappearances that took place. What happened?

Satan's Lie

Satan's man, the great world leader who will one day be revealed as Antichrist, will be quick with a lie to explain. Most likely, he will say that the ones left behind have the true Christ spirit. The ones who disappeared—at least the ones who disappeared who thought they were Christians—were mistaken. This great deceiver will likely reverse the truth in the matter of who is and who is not a true Christian.

After all, those who disappeared, he will say, were bigoted and narrow-minded. They believed that if you were a Buddhist, a Hindu, a Muslim, or whatever, you were not fit for Heaven. What kind of God would deny entrance into His Heaven just because of your religious beliefs?

Antichrist Will Call Rapture a Ruse

This is at least one explanation scenario Antichrist might use to make the "Christians" who are left behind feel better about themselves. The Rapture, he will probably say, was a total fraud. The disappearances had nothing to do with some Rapture that certain fanatics thought they had found within the Scriptures.

Soon after the Church is raptured, if not immediately following the event, many people will begin seriously reassessing their spiritual situations. They will remember, as did the protagonist Rayford Steele of the *Left Behind* series, that a wife, a son, a daughter, uncle, aunt—or someone—believed fervently in a coming Rapture. This remembrance will haunt them, and from this will grow an opening for God's salvation super sales force to begin a sales campaign for souls unlike any other evangelistic crusade that has ever been!

Second Chance?

This raises a question, no doubt, in the minds of many who believe
that there are no second chances for salvation once the Tribulation
begins. God's Word says that God himself will send (or allow)
strong delusion to come upon unbelievers at this time, and that
those who didn't believe before the Tribulation began will believe
Antichrist's lies. They will, in effect, never again be open to accepting the message. This is a tough one to figure. God's Word does indeed say just that.

An Answer?

Perhaps the answer lies in the very character of God. Jesus said: "All
that the Father gives Me will come to Me, and the one who comes to
Me I will by no means cast out" (John 6:37).

These two Bible truths concerning salvation seem to contradict
each other. One prophetic Bible truth says that all who did not believe before the Tribulation began will believe Antichrist's lie. They
will be forever lost. This is thought to mean that those so condemned understood perfectly the salvation message, but absolutely
refused to accept God's way.

That Scripture says: "And then the lawless one will be revealed,
whom the Lord will consume with the breath of His mouth and destroy with the brightness of His coming. The coming of the lawless
one is according to the working of Satan, with all power, signs, and
lying wonders, and with all unrighteous deception among those who
perish, because they did not receive the love of the truth, that they
might be saved. And for this reason God will send them strong delu-

sion, that they should believe the lie, that they all may be condemned who did not believe the truth but had pleasure in unrighteousness" (2 Thessalonians 2:8–12).

On the other hand, God said through the Apostle Peter: "The Lord is not slack concerning His promise, as some count slackness, but is long-suffering toward us, not willing that any should perish but that all should come to repentance" (2 Peter 3:9).

Which is it? What is the answer? Is there a second chance, or not?

A Matter of Timing

A possible, even probable, answer to the seeming contradiction is that there will be a time lapse between the Rapture and the beginning of the Tribulation. The Rapture of the Church doesn't start the Tribulation. Israel's signing the peace covenant that the Antichrist brokers initiates that last seven years of human history.

The "strong delusion" of 2 Thessalonians 2:8–12 is scheduled, prophetically, to take place in the Tribulation. There will likely be a time between the Rapture and the Tribulation's beginning, during which many who have heard and understood the salvation message but refused to accept Jesus Christ for salvation will understand what has happened and will become true Christians. They will not yet have come under the deluding influence of Satan's and his henchmen's lies.

Fleeting Last Chance?

That window of opportunity for belief after the Rapture will likely not be open for long. We can believe this because of the movement today toward a forced peace between Israel and her hostile neighbors. The peace covenant of Daniel 9:27 will most assuredly be on the drawing board ready for implementation by the time Christ calls His Church. It is not wise for a person to wait until that post-Rapture interlude to decide for Christ!

GOD'S DYNAMIC DUO

Once the great world leader who will soon become the full-fledged Antichrist signs the false peace covenant, guaranteeing Israel's security, the Tribulation will begin.

Satan's power will grow on Earth as God takes His mighty hand off the planet to some extent. The devil's pawns, the false-prophet religious leader and the world leader (Antichrist), will begin a propaganda blitz that will make Nazi propaganda look like bedtime stories by comparison.

Delusion, but Deliverance

God said that He will allow the minds of those who refused to accept Christ before the Tribulation to be deluded by the great lies the Antichrist regime will put forth. But God, being God, is merciful and compassionate, and more powerful than Satan and all his forces of evil. He will have ready the two witnesses of the salvation message, who will transfix the entire world with their preaching.

They will proclaim Jesus to be Israel's Messiah, and the only way to redemption from sin. They will also, no doubt, warn of the doom of all who follow Antichrist. The message will be powerful, clear, and plainly understood by every person who hears it. And with the tremendous communications networking around the globe, most everyone will doubtless hear their incessant preaching.

Power of Plagues

These strangely dressed men will have God's power to bring plagues upon Earth in the same manner Moses was given that authority during the time just before the Israelite exodus from Egypt.

Antichrist and his government will want to murder them. But God will supernaturally protect them while they constantly preach the message of salvation. As Bible prophecy says, they will preach for 1,260 days. Thousands, maybe millions, will hear and believe their words. Antichrist will be desperate to get rid of them. So will the rest of the world's people who believe that the great world leader, not God, is the answer to all their problems.

God's Ministers Murdered

Finally, when the two prophets' sermonizing has run its prophesied course, God will allow the Antichrist forces to kill them. They will lie in the streets of Jerusalem for three days, with all of the major networks' TV cameras trained upon their corpses. God's prophetic Word foretells the whole story of these strange witnesses:

"When they finish their testimony, the beast that ascends out of the bottomless pit will make war against them, overcome them, and kill them. And their dead bodies will lie in the street of the great city which spiritually is called Sodom and Egypt, where also our Lord was crucified. Then those from the peoples, tribes, tongues, and nations will see their dead bodies three-and-a-half days, and not allow their dead bodies to be put into graves. And those who dwell on the earth will rejoice over them, make merry, and send gifts to one another, because these two prophets tormented those who dwell on the earth. Now after the three-and-a-half days breath of life from God entered them, and they stood on their feet, and great fear fell on those who saw them. And they heard a loud voice from heaven saying to them, 'Come up here.' And they ascended to heaven in a cloud, and their enemies saw them" (Revelation 11:7–12).

Notice the Bible says that Antichrist and most of all of the rest of the world will be so gleeful that they've finally been able to kill these two men, that they will actually throw parties and send gifts to one another in celebration. Then, with the whole world watching by satellite and other means, the prophets will come to life, stand to their feet, and be taken to Heaven. Imagine the fear that will blacken the mood of all of those who are in the middle of their drunken celebrations!

Instantaneous Turning to God

This resurrection and ascension will undoubtedly cause many people to instantly repent of their sins and accept the message the pair had been preaching. Antichrist's learning of such a great mass conversion to true Christianity will drive him more insane than ever. Persecution of the Christians, and of the Jews, will increase exponentially from that point.

GOD'S SUPER SALES TEAM

God will not stand by and allow Satan to have completely free rein when it comes to the matter of souls. The two witnesses will be taken into Heaven, but the Lord will have ready a salvation sales team that will bring millions to conversion to Christ. The prophet John recorded the prophecy about these mighty evangelists: "Then I saw another angel ascending from the east, having the seal of the living God. And he cried with a loud voice to the four angels to whom it was granted to harm the earth and the sea, saying, 'Do not harm the earth, the sea, or the trees till we have sealed the servants of our God on their foreheads.' And I heard the number of those who were sealed. One hundred and forty-four thousand of all the tribes of the children of Israel were sealed" (Revelation 7:2–4).

Seal of God

These people will be sealed with God's seal in their foreheads. This is the opposite of Antichrist's mark, which dooms all who take it to eternity apart from God. God's mark in the 144,000 preachers' foreheads assures they will spend eternity with God, and that they will be physically protected by Him during the time they are sharing God's message.

All-Israeli Sales Force

Revelation 7:5–8 tells that twelve thousand people will be taken from each tribe of the twelve tribes of Israel to serve as preachers of the Gospel of Christ and the kingdom of God. Judgments are not to begin from Heaven until these 144,000 are sealed, so the sealing will take place very early in the Tribulation.

These Jewish people, who have been converted to belief in Jesus, will be the most powerful speakers for the cause of Christ in the history of Christian evangelism. They will have to be. The odds against becoming a true believer in Jesus Christ during this era will be greatly stacked against the populations of Earth for two reasons:

1. The deception and "strong delusion" of 2 Thessalonians, chapter 2, will be oppressing all people.
2. Those who do choose Christ over Antichrist will face being murdered. Most who become Christians will be martyred, the Scriptures prophesy.

Most Martyred

Millions will accept the message the 144,000 preach, and most will die for their faith.

The fact that millions will accept Christ during that era is a testimony to God's profound love and amazing grace and to the total devotion these 144,000 salvation super salesmen will bring to their cause.

THE MARTYRED AND THE MARKED

God's evangelists will present the salvation message, and millions will buy. Those who purchase that heavenly product will possess something that will last for eternity. Actually, it is Jesus who will have purchased their souls for them. He paid for them with His blood, a commodity that God views as the most precious and valuable in all of His vast kingdom.

In contrast to the Tribulation saints (those who accept Christ during that era), the rest of the citizens of Antichrist's world will buy his mark in order to survive. The mark will, in some way, include the mysterious number of the beast's name. That number is, as we know, 666.

Those who accept his mark—which will undoubtedly be part of a super-technological economic system of some sort—will have sold their souls to buy a few more weeks, months, or years of life. But, sadly, their souls are forever lost, once their decision to accept Satan's mark is made.

The Martyrs

People who refuse to take Antichrist's mark will face great suffering and death. These will be cut out of the system of buying and selling. Their credit will be no good—that's one mild way to say it. There will be no government poverty programs for them. Anyone caught helping them in any way will, themselves, face the wrath of Antichrist's police forces.

People refusing the mark of the beast will be telling Antichrist (and Satan, who literally possesses him) that they will not worship him. The punishment for this, according to Bible prophecy, will be having their heads lopped off.

Their suffering will be horrible, but brief when compared to the eternity of suffering those who choose to take the mark of the beast will face.

REVELATION 7:9-17

John the apostle and prophet saw a vision in which millions upon millions of people wearing white robes stood before God's throne, and God, the Son. They had palm leaves in their hands and were praising God the Father and God the Son. When one of the people there, called an elder, asked John who these millions of people were, John could only say he didn't know, but that the elder knew. The elder then told John these were the people who had been killed during the Tribulation. Their giving up their lives for Christ's sake during those terrible days meant they stood before God as sinless, and were greatly beloved. They will never suffer again, but will enjoy the pleasures of Heaven, being eternally in God's presence. Jesus, himself, will see to it they will never again suffer. God will see to it that they never shed another tear.

The Marked

Life will be anything but pleasant for the citizens of Satan's version of Utopia. They will worship a god who ultimately will bring suffering even more terrible than that inflicted upon the martyrs for Christ. When God's direct judgments begin to fall, suffering on Planet Earth will be unprecedented (*Find It Fast:* Revelation 14:9–11).

When God's salesmen come calling on the left-behind people of Planet Earth during the Tribulation, the buying decision will be a matter of eternal life or death. It's one decision you won't have to make if you're Rapture ready!

END-TIME AILMENTS AND RAPTURE-READY RX

Conspirarrhea A chronic and progressive problem in which the subject begins to care more about conspiracies than about the more obvious problems of life. He begins to lose trust in God's power, believing that the imagined conspirators are the ones calling all the shots.

Symptoms These folks often believe they are being watched by agents of the government or secret organizations. They frequently subscribe to several conspiracy theories.

Treatment These people need to refocus their energies in the right direction. They give the enemy too much credit and need to focus on the power of God: "For we do not wrestle against flesh and blood, but against principalities, against powers, against the rulers of the darkness of this age, against spiritual hosts of wickedness in the heavenly places" (Ephesians 6:12).

IT'S A WORLD
WITHOUT END
WHEN GOD IS
YOUR FRIEND!

CHAPTER 14

It's the End of
the World As We Know It

"Cameron tells me he does not know one common citizen who does not own and carry a weapon. I hardly hear from countries where there are not marauding bands of thieves and rapists, not to mention vandals and terrorists. The best things we have out there are the 144,000 evangelists and the increase in angelic activity the Lord has so graciously allowed.

"Remember, Rayford, we are down to three kinds of people now: those of us with the mark of God, those who bear the mark of Antichrist, and the undecided. There are fewer and fewer of these, but they are the ones we must reach out to. They are suffering now, but oh, how they will suffer as the sun rises each day. Imagine the turmoil, the devastation. Power shortages, air conditioning overloads, breakdowns. And all this coming with half of the population already gone."

—*The Remnant* (Wheaton, Illinois: Tyndale, 2002)

FOR A HOT TIME—CALL 666!

One judgment that will come upon the Earth, thanks to Mr. 666 and those who worship him, is that God will cause the sun to become many times hotter than normal. Even though men will be scorched by the intensity, they still will curse God and refuse to repent of their sin and rebellion (*Find It Fast*: Revelation 16:8–9).

FIND
IT
FAST

More than five years into the Tribulation, Rayford Steele listens to an assessment of the dire circumstances all around. Even the murderously oppressive Antichrist government can't control the human tidal wave of evil assaulting a dying world. Neither can Antichrist nor anyone else combat the great heat and other plagues that are the judgments of God upon blasphemous, rebellious people.

That novel account points to the long-feared end of the world talked about and written about throughout history. Although the *Left Behind* series book *The Remnant* is fiction, it's on-target about, or perhaps even underestimates, the way things will unfold at that point in the Apocalypse.

Today's Troubles

Today, every major event that shocks us makes it seem that our world will never again be the same. We can say that, in one sense, it's the end of the world as we know it, each time something so profoundly affects the world. Everything surrounding our lives now seems a little bit more ominous. The future looks bleaker, and things will never again be as they were before.

Some such events in modern times in America include the 1929 stock market crash, the Japanese attack on Pearl Harbor, the sudden death of wartime president Franklin Roosevelt, the advent of the atomic bomb, the Cuban missile crisis, the assassination of President John F. Kennedy, the explosion of the space shuttle *Challenger,* and the 2001 terrorist attacks on New York and Washington, D.C. These events, shocking though they were, are mild compared to the things Bible prophecy predicts will happen during the few years of history before Christ returns. The last three and one-half years will make it seem that, indeed, it is the end of the world.

Anxious Seek Answers

Anxiety grows during crises. People look for answers to what has happened, and what is likely to be the result of what has happened. In most every case, people turn instinctively to the spiritual realm for answers, and for comfort. This was true, as stated before, when the churches swelled in attendance following the terrorist attacks of September 11, 2001.

FEARFUL OF FUTURE

Interest in prophecy, whether biblical or otherwise, inevitably seems to surface at times of national and world crises. People don't usually openly state their fear of an end-of-the-world scenario, but that fear runs as an undercurrent below the crises events when they are severe enough.

War Worries

The Gulf War and Desert Storm of 1990 instantly raised fears of Armageddon. Armageddon always is a hot topic whenever the Middle East is involved. Israel evokes thoughts of Bible prophecy and of the Second Coming, and particularly of the battle of Armageddon.

When the Scud missiles started flying toward that ancient and at the same time modern nation, even the normally nonreligious media commentators displayed a bit of end-of-the-world jitters. Everybody seemed to breathe sighs of relief when Israel chose to go along with President George H. W. Bush and not retaliate against Saddam Hussein when he sent the deadly Scuds toward the tiny state.

Prophecy scholars were suddenly in demand for interviews when that technological storm of military might began lighting up our television screens. Questions often came up that asked whether this could be the beginning of Armageddon, and thus the underlying question: Is this the end of the world?

Well, Is It?

Authorities on true Bible prophecy answer that question the same way: No. The world will go on forever. Prophecy teachers explain over and over that they don't preach that the world will come to an end.

Earth's Certain Survival

FIND IT FAST

Bible prophecy describes the resilience of our world, which will stagger "like a drunkard" under the hand of God as He sends unparalleled judgments (*Find it Fast:* Isaiah 24:20). But the physical sphere called Earth will survive: "One generation passes away, and another generation comes; But the earth abides forever" (Ecclesiastes 1:4).

The big blue marble, then, is prophesied to be down, but not out. That's because it's opponent in the end-time battle—in the battle of the ages—will reach down and lift it and make it as if it had never fallen. God, the Creator of all things, will make all things new, Bible prophecy says.

BIG BATTLE

Before that happens, though, a tremendous battle between good and evil must be fought. Each round will become progressively bloodier. Actually, the opposing forces are already in the ring. The arena is filled with participants, and all alive at the time the fight unfolds will suffer from the battle.

Many will have left the building by the time the bell of Apocalypse rings. These will escape the effects of the fight by way of the Rapture. This ultimate battle of good against evil is for the title deed to Planet Earth. The fight is prophesied to be fought for twenty-one rounds. These are twenty-one judgments in a series of three portions: the seal judgments, the trumpet judgments, and the bowl or vial judgments. Jesus alone directs the judgments.

THE SEAL JUDGMENTS

The four horsemen of the Apocalypse will ride forth upon command by Jesus, as He unrolls each of the first four sealed scrolls. These will be the opening rounds of this bloody battle.

Round One: White Horse of False Peace
(Revelation 6:2)

The first rider, on the white horse, is Antichrist, who will come offering peace. As we've already discussed, he is really a deceiver and a conqueror, however.

Round Two: Red Horse of War
(Revelation 6:4)

The second rider, on a red horse, is the rider of war. The false peace Antichrist promised will be broken, and millions will die from unprecedented wars.

Round Three: Black Horse of Famine
(Revelation 6:5)

The third rider, on a black horse, is famine. Millions upon millions will die of starvation and other results of the all-out war making ushered in by the rider on the red horse.

Round Four: Pale Horse of Death
(Revelation 6:8)

The fourth rider, on a pale horse, has a partner riding close behind. The front rider is death. Sheol, the abode of the dead nonbelievers, will follow. These riders will account for the death of one-fourth of the world's population.

Round Five: Martyrs (Revelation 6:9–11)

When Jesus opens the fifth seal, the saints of the Tribulation era who have been martyred for Christ will be seen in their white robes of salvation before God's throne.

Round Six: Earth-Shaking Events
(Revelation 6:12–14)

As the sixth seal is opened, there will be a great earthquake, the sun will darken, and the moon will turn red. These events will so frighten the leaders of Earth that they will beg the rocks and caves in which they are hiding to fall on them, and conceal them from the furious God of Heaven.

Round Seven: Getting a Breather
(Revelation 8:1–2)

Unlike human athletes, God needs no breaks to catch His breath. But He seems to take a breather in anticipation of the next catastrophic set of judgments with the opening of the seventh seal: a thirty-minute period of silence in Heaven. Following that quiet time, seven angels standing before God will be given the seven trumpets.

THE TRUMPET JUDGMENTS

God then prepares to step up the pace of judgment against the foolish Earth dwellers as the trumpet judgments begin.

Round Eight (First Trumpet): Hail, Fire, and Blood (Revelation 8:6–7)

After the angel sounds the first trumpet, hail and fire mixed with blood will fall from Heaven. The fire will cause all green grass and a third of the Earth's trees to burn up. Certainly, it will already appear to be the end of the world as we know it. God will fire off a stunning blow to those who will not repent of their sin against Him. But this will be just the beginning of His body blows to the planet.

Round Nine (Second Trumpet): Burning Mountain (Revelation 8:8–9)

Something that appeared to John to look like a burning mountain will be cast into the sea. A third of the sea will turn to blood, a third of all sea life will die, and a third of the ships at sea will be destroyed.

This will be a stupendous blow to a planet already reeling because of God's judgments. Anytime God's Word uses phrases like "as it were" (Revelation 8:8), it is a symbolic description to show something that is literal. In other words, this will not be a literal mountain, but it will be "like" a mountain in size. It really will be a big rock that's on fire, and it sounds much like the asteroids, meteors, and other rocks from space that pose danger to our planet. This prophecy appears to forewarn that something like that will slam into one of Earth's oceans.

This event will be catastrophic to Earth's environment, because the Bible says that the sea will become like blood, thick and slimy—apparently like blood plasma. A third of sea life will die and a third of all ships will be destroyed by the tremendous tidal waves.

Round Ten (Third Trumpet): Star Called Wormwood (Revelation 8:10–11)

A heavenly object of some sort called "Wormwood" will cause another great blow to Earth's water supplies as it crashes into the planet. This time the fresh waters will be poisoned, and people who drink from the affected waters will die.

Round Eleven (Fourth Trumpet): Darkness (Revelation 8:12)

The Earth's inhabitants will next receive a black eye, so to speak, so that their vision will be severely affected. The sun will darken by one-third, so naturally the moon, a reflective body, will also have its light diminished by one-third. The stars also will be supernaturally darkened (*Find It Fast:* Revelation 8:12).

God seems to step back and size up His opponent before moving in to punish the rebels of Earth even more. The ringside announcer—an angel—will announce that the next judgments will be even worse than the first (*Find It Fast:* Revelation 8:13).

Round Twelve (Fifth Trumpet):
Plague of Locusts

God apparently allows an angelic being to open the abyss, or "bottomless pit," releasing the weirdest, most fearsome creatures ever seen on Earth (*Find It Fast:* Revelation 9:1–5). They are described as being like scorpions whose stings hurt people for five months. Many prophecy scholars are convinced the angelic being is Satan, who will fall to Earth when he is cast out of Heaven during the Tribulation, and that the creatures are a horde of demons.

Round Thirteen (Sixth Trumpet):
Army of Evil Horsemen (Revelation 9:15–21)

God will order the unbinding of demonic beings, whose habitation is somewhere beneath the Euphrates River. These are angels who followed Lucifer in his original rebellion against the Lord. They apparently will enter into and possess the 200 million troops that come from the Orient, which is east of the Euphrates. These tremendous numbers are referred to as "the kings of the East" in Revelation 16:12.

The might of these forces will be awesome. They will inflict horrific damage on all in their path. Another one-third of the people left on the Earth will die because of their war making. Still, no one will repent and bow before God

Round Fourteen (Seventh Trumpet):
Heralding the Bowl Judgments
(Revelation 10–15)

Again, God will pause in His assault on His evil opponents. He will stop between the sixth and seventh trumpet judgments to tell all the things that will take place between the blowing of the sixth trumpet and the beginning of the vial, or bowl, judgments. These awesome prophetic events include the two witnesses' time on the Tribulation scene; the 144,000 sealed super evangelists; the whole story of

Satan's hatred for Jesus and the Jewish race, and the rise and fall of Antichrist.

Round Fifteen (Bowl One): Sores
(Revelation 16:2)

The next assault will begin with the pouring out of the first of the seven deadly bowls of the pure wrath of the living God. Unbelievably horrible sores will infect all who have rejected God.

Round Sixteen (Bowl Two): Bloody Sea
(Revelation 16:3)

Before they switched to twelve-rounders as maximum, the fifteenth round in a world championship fight was the last one. In this battle of the ages, the fight will be just getting heated up. And it will be one-sided. Judgments from the Lord are so frightful, the prophet John must have had to totally depend upon the Lord for the words to describe them: "Then the second angel poured out his bowl on the sea, and it became blood as of a dead man; and every living creature in the sea died."

God's Word, through John, doesn't even attempt to describe what will be poured into the sea. But it will kill every living thing, whatever it is. The water will become like a dead man's blood. Imagine! Water with the viscosity and, apparently, the stench and grotesqueness of coagulating blood.

Round Seventeen (Bowl Three): Bloody Rivers (Revelation 16:4)

The third angel will pour out his bowl into the fresh waters, and they will turn to blood. The judgments are indeed fearsome, but God is totally righteous in inflicting them upon the inhabitants of Earth who have rejected Him. We hear the voices from God's corner urging him onward, as the fight continues: "You are righteous, O Lord, the one who is and who was and who is to be, because You have judged these things. For they have shed the blood of saints and prophets, and You have given them blood to drink. For it is their just due" (Revelation 16:5–6).

Round Eighteen (Bowl Four): Scorching Heat (Revelation 16:8–9)

God will pound the Earth with heavier and heavier blows. As the fourth angel pours out his bowl on the sun, it apparently goes into partial nova. That is, it will shrink and grow darker. Yet at the same time, it will get much hotter. Men cannot escape the scorching, killing heat. Rather than beg for forgiveness, they will curse God's holy name!

Round Nineteen (Bowl Five): Darkness and Pain (Revelation 16:10–11)

God pours His judgments directly upon the most rebellious of the rebels. Apparently, ultraviolet rays from the dying sun will laser

PAUSE FOR THE BIG FINISH

Before the seventh bowl will be poured out, Almighty God pauses to say something about those who are His own: "Behold, I am coming as a thief. Blessed is he who watches, and keeps his garments, lest he walk naked and they see his shame." And they gathered them together to the place called, in Hebrew, Armageddon. Then the seventh angel poured out his bowl into the air, and a loud voice came out of the temple of Heaven, from the throne, saying, "It is done!" (Revelation 16:15–17).

He seems to cover all from the Church Age through the Tribulation who are Christians. His words for Church Age saints seem to commend them for watching for Christ's any-moment return. He says He will come unannounced and suddenly upon an unsuspecting world. He will come "as a thief" because it will be an unanticipated, unwelcome break-in upon the world of rebels who do not know or want Him.

His own, however, should be watching for Him. They shouldn't be surprised by an unwelcome break-in upon their lives. They should never be comfortable with living like the rest of the world.

He gives blessings to the Tribulation saints for keeping their robes of righteousness by being faithful to Him. They did so in the face of the rebels who wanted to see them disrobe—that is, to deny Christ.

through Earth's unprotected atmosphere and cause skin eruptions on those not sealed with God's protection. They will gnaw their tongues in agony, but when they do manage to speak intelligible words, they will speak curses against the Lord.

Round Twenty (Bowl Six): Euphrates Dries Up (Revelation 16:12)

Next, God will allow total demonic activity to take place upon Earth. The vilest demonic spirits apparently will be unleashed in the area of the Euphrates River. These spirits will enter into the military forces of the world, and tremendous death and destruction from the great campaign called Armageddon (for it is a war campaign, not just a single, final battle) will intensify by the minute (Revelation 16:12–14).

The hordes from the Orient called "the kings of the east" will be allowed easy access to the Middle East because the Euphrates River, a natural barrier to land forces, is dried up.

Round Twenty-One (Bowl Seven): Greatest of all Earthquakes and Hundred-Pound Hailstones (Revelation 16:18–20)

The final tremendous blow from God's great right hand of judgment—following His weighty words, "It is done"—will come in the form of a devastating earthquake and giant hailstones that flatten every city on the planet. Jerusalem will split into three parts. Entire islands will disappear under the titanic blow. What could stand under the pounding of hailstones that weigh more than one hundred pounds each? The rebels are literally pounded into submission in this final round of judgments. The Babylonian system of godless humanism, commercialism, and religion will come to an end (*Find It Fast:* Revelation, chapters 17 and 18).

FIND
IT
FAST

It really isn't much of a fight, is it? To put it in juvenile fight language: "There wasn't really but two punches thrown." God hits His enemies, and His enemies hit the ground.

JESUS WILL REJUVENATE

As devastated as Planet Earth will be after the apocalyptic horrors it will go through, it will still be in existence. Christ will personally pick it up, dust it off, and make it Heaven on Earth. That's something Antichrist had falsely promised the deluded rebels who worshipped him by accepting his mark. After the millennial reign of Christ, the Earth will undergo even further renovation.

Planetary Purification

For the record, Revelation does talk about the Earth being renewed after the millennium. This will be a planned event, not a spontaneous one. A number of Scriptures assure us the Earth will exist forever:

- ⊕ Isaiah 45:17—"But Israel shall be saved by the Lord with an everlasting salvation; you shall not be ashamed or disgraced forever and ever."
- ⊕ Ecclesiastes 1:4—"One generation passes away, and another generation comes; but the earth abides forever."
- ⊕ Psalm 104:5—"You who laid the foundations of the earth, so that it should not be moved forever."

⊕ Ephesians 3:21—"To Him be glory in the church by Christ Jesus to all generations, forever and ever. Amen."

⊕ Isaiah 9:6—"For unto us a Child is born, unto us a Son is given; and the government will be upon His shoulders. And his name will be called Wonderful, Counselor, Mighty God, Everlasting Father, Prince of Peace."

⊕ Isaiah 9:7—"Of the increase of His government and peace there will be no end, upon the throne of David and over His kingdom, to order it and establish it with judgment and justice from that time forward, even forever. The zeal of the Lord of hosts will perform this."

Barely the Beginning

The Earth as we presently know it will soon come to an end. But the world to come for those who are true believers in Jesus Christ will be far better than was Planet Earth at its best. Best of all, it will be a world that will never end. The line in the old hymn "Amazing Grace" is appropriate: "When we've been there ten thousand years, bright shining as the sun, we've no less days to sing God's praise, than when we've first begun."

A good enough reason to be Rapture ready!

END-TIME AILMENTS AND RAPTURE-READY RX

Wrath of God Rash When suffering from this ailment, people claim that all calamities are part of God's end-time judgment. They believe every negative occurrence is wrath being poured out by the Almighty.

Symptoms Has a "they-had-it-coming" attitude regarding tragic events. Feels frustrated when hurricanes, tornadoes, and earthquakes miss striking populated areas.

Treatment Needs to realize that until Judgment Day, God still blesses the wicked and the good. "That you may be sons of your Father in heaven; for He makes His sun rise on the evil and on the good, and sends rain on the just and on the unjust" (Matthew 5:45).

YOU DON'T
HAVE TO FEAR
WHEN JESUS
IS NEAR!

CHAPTER 15

Jesus Is Coming; Everybody Look Busy!

Chloe had grown quiet. "Whatcha thinking?" he said.

She pursed her lips, and buried her hands in her jacket pockets.

"About what fun we would have had if we'd been lovers at any other time in history."

He nodded. "We wouldn't have been believers."

"Someone might have gotten to us. Look at us. This is the most fun I've had in ages. It's like we're in a free car dealership, and it's our turn to pick. We've got a beautiful baby and a free sitter, and all we have to do is decide what model and color car we want."

She rested against a white Hummer and Buck joined her. She shook her head. "We're older than our years, wounded, scarred, scared. It won't be long before our days will be spent looking for ways to just stay alive. I worry about you all the time. It's bad enough living now, but, I couldn't go on without you."

"Yes you could."

"I wouldn't want to. Would you, without me? Maybe I shouldn't ask."

"No, Chlo', I know what you mean. We have a cause, a mission, and everything seems crystal clear. But I wouldn't want to go on without you either. I *would*. I'd *have* to. For Kenny. For God. For the rest of the Force. Like Tsion says, for the kingdom. You'd have been the best thing that ever happened to me even if you weren't my whole life. But you are. Let's watch out for each other, keep each other alive. We've got only three and a half years to go, but I want to make it. Don't you?"

" 'Course."

She turned and held him tightly for a long minute, and they kissed fiercely.

—*The Mark* (Wheaton, Illinois, Tyndale, 2000)

BUSINESS AS NOT SO USUAL

Buck and Chloe, main characters in *The Mark,* are married now and have a baby. They also fight covertly against Antichrist's regime. Life is anything but business as usual three and one-half years into the Tribulation.

Their business is God's business. Their goal is to see as many souls as possible turn to Christ during the most terrible time of persecution against Jews and Christians in history.

Despite being believers with a mission they fervently work to carry out, their love for each other and passion for surviving until

Christ's Second Coming three and a half years away occupy all of their thoughts. It must be that way. Their lives depend on being constantly alert, and staying on the offensive against the devil's forces.

They work also for Christ because they want to hear Him say, when they are at last in His presence, "Well done, good and faithful servants."

FACT MORE THAN FICTION

The above scenario involving these fictional characters isn't far-fetched. A very similar scene will likely play out for real in the not too distant future. We can say this with earnest conviction because God's Word says through the prophet Daniel that Antichrist will flatter—with congratulatory words and with spoils of his regime's plunder—those who hate and persecute the Jews and believers in Christ. The beast will be powerful, but the Bible says believers will be empowered by God, and will do great "exploits" (*Find It Fast*: Daniel 11:32).

FIND IT FAST

All who follow Christ at that time will be forced to struggle greatly against the Antichrist monsters, or they will not live long. There will be no room for laziness and unfaithfulness to the cause of Jesus in that apocalyptic era. Even though much of their resistance and attempts to reach others for Christ will be carried on in secret, Bible prophecy says their exploits will be tremendous. Their deeds will be considered great in God's eyes, because they will struggle against fearful and overwhelming odds.

SUPERNATURAL HELP

God won't leave His saints of the apocalypse to go through hell on Earth without His assistance. He will send special help to those of the Tribulation time:

1. Gift of Prophecy

"And it shall come to pass in the last days, says God, that I will pour out of My Spirit on all flesh; your sons and your daughters shall prophesy. Your young men shall see visions, your old men shall dream dreams" (Acts 2:17). The Lord, in His great love, will give His children the gifts of foretelling so that His people can manipulate their way successfully through the Tribulation maze of hatred against them. God's children will have supernatural prophecy gifts. Young men will see visions. They will look into the future to see things that might harm believers and the cause of Christ. They also will be urged on by the fantastic promises they see awaiting believers when Christ returns.

Old men will dream dreams. These will be encouraged, and encourage others by the magnificent things they will dream about what God has prepared for those believers who go through the Tribulation.

2. Energy to Endure

Times will be so desperately oppressive and dangerous that believers will need supernatural energy to survive: "And ye will be hated by all for My name's sake. But he who endures to the end shall be saved" (Mark 13:13).

BELIEVERS KEEPING BUSY

Despite the terrors of that last three and one-half years, just before Jesus comes back to take over Planet Earth, believers will be more productive for Christ than believers of any other time. They will know exactly when their Lord is coming back. The precise time of Christ's return can be figured exactly once the seven-year Tribulation period begins.

Believers on Earth will want to please God, and to bring as many people into His kingdom as possible. That's what every Christian of every era should be about: planting the seeds of the Gospel—giving the message that Jesus died, was buried, and resurrected for the payment of sin—so that God can reap a soul harvest.

Christians of the Tribulation won't have to be urged: "Everybody look busy, Jesus is coming!" They will be too busy on His behalf to have too many pep rallies!

ATTENTION, CHRISTIANS!

On the other hand, there is definitely a need for a pep rally or two today! Jesus is indeed coming. The signals are everywhere. This generation, unlike those Tribulation era people, doesn't know the exact time of His return, but we are told to know the times and seasons of His coming in the Rapture for His Church. In other words, Christians alive during this pre-Rapture time are to watch and understand that the end-time signs are right in front of our eyes, no matter which direction we turn.

Jesus said: "And what I say to you, I say unto all: Watch!" (Mark 13:37).

BUSY BUSYBODIES

Unfortunately, in this tremendous time of signs that God has granted our generation, Christians are too often engaged in busybody business, not real business, for the Lord. Churches split over ridiculous matters. Believers backbite and gossip about other believers, all to the harm of the cause of Jesus, whose business in coming was not to provide a comfortable church setting from which to sit and snipe at others, but to bring men, women, and children to salvation.

"I'M A BETTER CHRISTIAN THAN YOU" (BY THE HOLIER-THAN-THOU COMMITTEE)

Far too often, some Christians today sit and look snootily down their noses at others, whose sins they view as much greater than their own mere "mistakes." One of the most effective deceptions that Satan has foisted upon Christians is this idea that certain groups are more spiritually mature than less-enlightened believers. The endless game of "I am more approved in the Lord's eyes than you" divides the Church and gives nonbelievers a negative picture of the Christian faith.

Few people would ever openly say, "I'm a better Christian than you." It is through their beliefs and deeds that they proclaim their superiority. Here are a few common ways people promote spiritual elitism.

1. **The "One True Church"**
   The trademark of this belief is that a particular group has a stranglehold on the truth and that there is no salvation outside

Mark 7:9—"He said unto them, 'All too well you reject the commandment of God, that you may keep your tradition.'"

of their organization. They hold that their leaders are specially anointed by God, in many cases infallible in interpretation, and, more importantly, are above reproach. They place their beliefs in what they feel are superior interpretations of Scripture and are more concerned about the doctrines and traditions of man than the Word of God. This factor is also very common with cults. The appeal of the group is the honor of being part of an exclusive club.

Special "revelations from God" are the trademark of those who claim to be the God-anointed of the "one true Church," but are not. These types of leaders frequently try to hype their supposed uniqueness by predicting upcoming events. Because only God knows the future, these false revelations are guaranteed to fail. The Bible requires a 100 percent accuracy rate for all predictions that are claimed to have originated from God.

One-true-churchism leads people to doubt their salvation and spend more time worrying about their actions than on the Word of God and their personal walk with Him.

2. The Keepers of the Law

This group of people believes in keeping Torah observance. While people may choose to keep the Levitical dietary laws or the Sabbath, there is a fine line between personal choice and self-righteousness.

This group maintains that Jesus never intended for the law to go away, basing the belief on Matthew 5:17: "Do not think that I came to destroy the law . . ." and John 14:15: "If you love Me, keep My commandments."

What they are missing, however, is that Jesus clarified what He was referring to and it had nothing to do with the Old Testament laws. When Jesus was cornered by the Pharisees and asked which of the commandments were the greatest, He replied: "You shall love the Lord your God with all your heart, with all your soul, and with all your mind. This is the first and greatest commandment. And the second is like it: 'You shall love your neighbor as yourself.' On these two commandments hang all the Law and the Prophets" (Matthew 22:37–40).

What was He referencing? Isaiah 29:13: "Therefore the Lord said: 'Inasmuch as these people draw near with their mouths and honor Me with their lips, but have removed their hearts far from Me, and their fear toward Me is taught by the commandment of men,'" and Jeremiah 31:33: "But this is the covenant that I will make with the house of Israel after those days, says the Lord: I will put My law in their minds, and write it on their hearts; and I will be their God, and they shall be my people."

Galatians 5:4—"You have become estranged from Christ, you who attempt to be justified by law; you have fallen from grace."

It is impossible for the Judaic law to save anyone. The standard is too high for any to follow it to perfection. The law said, "You're not guilty if you don't do it." Jesus said, "You're guilty if you even think about doing something that is wrong." Paul warned us in Galatians that we can frustrate the grace of God by trying to follow after the law (*Find It Fast*: Galatians 2:21).

3. Legalists

Scripture tells us that we are to exhort fellow believers (*Find It Fast:* 1 Thessalonians 4:1). So where is the line between assisting fellow believers in their Christian lives and condemning them for their thoughts and actions?

FIND
IT
FAST

Common sense dictates believers should not dress wantonly and get drunk, but common sense is not enough for the legalist crowd. They feel that it is their duty to protect people from themselves, so they create measuring sticks in order to maintain their role as their brothers' keepers.

Based on 1 Thessalonians 5:22, which says that we should abstain from "all appearance" of evil, popular legalisms promoted are:

⊕ no drinking

⊕ no smoking

⊕ no dancing

⊕ no going to movies

⊕ no attending sporting events (because they sell beer)

⊕ no haircuts, jewelry, or slacks for women

⊕ no above-the-knee styles of women's skirts or culottes should be worn

⊕ no shorts for men, regardless of the weather

⊕ no eating out on Sundays

And besides all that, a minister must approve everything a person does. The list is endless.

While we are not advocating a freewheeling lifestyle, we are saying that we have been instructed simply to walk in the

> Matthew 23:24—"Blind guides, who strain out a gnat and swallow a camel!"

Lord's light. Our deeds are like filthy rags to God. The only thing that matters to Him is what's in our hearts.

Legalism pits one believer against another in an unending cycle of condemnation. Additionally, it can turn people away from understanding the grace of Christ when they are made to feel that they have bigger shoes to fill than they can wear.

4. KJV-Onlyism

Some Christians proclaim that the 1611 King James Version (KJV) is the one and only true English version of the Word of God. While the Rapture Ready Web site uses the KJV for quoting Scripture, it is only because this version is the most widely quoted. Nothing is dramatically wrong with some other Christian Bibles versions such as the NKJV (used in this book), New American Standard, and Revised Standard Versions. There are versions today, however, that in our opinion stray from the original to the extent they weaken the truth of God's Word. Be careful in selecting the version you use, is our advice.

Some versions of the Bible have been specifically rewritten to accommodate private interpretations. Examples include the Clear Word Bible of the Seventh-Day Adventists and the New World Translation of the Jehovah's Witnesses. We are strongly against recommending these in any way whatsoever.

The King James Version was written in Elizabethan English (à la Shakespeare) and can be rather difficult for some people to read, especially those new to the faith.

Hebrews 5:12—"For though by this time you ought to be teachers, you need someone to teach you again the first principles of the oracles of God; and you have come to need milk and not solid food."

5. Word of Faith Elitism

This group promotes the doctrine of "Name it and Claim it," which says that the Lord is holding a storehouse full of blessings in Heaven, just waiting for the faithful to claim their rewards while they're still here on Earth. They teach that those in the Lord's favor are blessed with health and wealth and that those who are struggling in life are not blessed because of their inferior relationship with the Lord and their lack of faith and trust in Him.

The biggest question here is the one of universal application. Is this teaching practical and accessible to all? Is a teaching from God's Word if it only applies to affluent suburbia but

Matthew 6:19–20—"Do not lay up for yourselves treasures on earth, where moth and rust destroy and where thieves break in and steal; but lay up for yourselves treasures in heaven, where neither moth nor rust destroys and where thieves do not break in and steal."

Mark 10:31—"But many who are first will be last, and the last first."

not to the underdeveloped nations of the world? What application does the teaching have for believers imprisoned for their faith by atheistic, Islamic, and other repressive governments?

"Word of faith" beliefs promote elitism between the "haves" and the "have nots" by claiming that those who "have not" aren't good enough Christians and the Lord is treating them as such.

6. The Intellectuals

One of the most basic human desires is for someone to seek after and receive the praise of mankind. Many Christians like to impress other believers with their intellectual capabilities. Some go as far as proclaiming themselves to be spiritually superior to anyone who does not share the same level of academic achievement.

The intellectual crowd causes great harm to the message of Christ. They motivate fellow Christians to strive to achieve a lofty vocabulary that is often above the heads of the average

1 Corinthians 3:18–19—"Let no one deceive himself. If any one among you seems to be wise in this age, let him become a fool that he may become wise. For the wisdom of this world is foolishness with God. For it is written, 'He catches the wise in their own craftiness.' "

Romans 1:21–22—"Because, although they knew God, they did not glorify Him as God, nor were thankful, but became futile in their thoughts, and their foolish hearts were darkened. Professing themselves to be wise, they became fools."

person. The general philosophy applies that it is better to appear to be intelligent than it is to be understood by your audience.

The Bible repeatedly warns against trusting in our own abilities for wisdom. Because Satan is a spirit being, with nearly unlimited intellectual skills, no man is able to match wits with him. Anyone who strays from the Word of God to rely on his own understanding is making a terrible mistake.

BOTTOM LINE

Individuals who hold to an "I'm a better Christian than you" mindset can always find Scripture to support their stance. They need to examine their rationale for holding to that view. If their offering of correction is not sparked from love, then one can conclude pride is their motivation.

These Christians should get busy being busy for Christ, not being busy being busybodies!

Philippians 2:2–3—"Fulfill my joy by being like-minded, having the same love, being of one accord, of one mind. Let nothing be done through selfish ambition or conceit, but in lowliness of mind let each esteem others better than himself."

CHRIST'S CATASTROPHIC COMING

Jesus Christ's coming will spell catastrophe for those who don't want Him to get involved in the lives of those living on Earth. The first phase of His Second Coming, as we have seen, will happen suddenly, and will inflict great changes for the people of Earth (although He won't immediately send judgments when He raptures the Church).

Certainly, many cultures will be in upheaval immediately following this event. Human government will, with the help of media and left-behind clergy, quickly restore societal equilibrium. The unparalleled disappearance disaster will present the perfect opportunity for the world to come together as one. At last, there will be unity, a common denominator to formulate the equation for the peace that has so long been sought.

COMING AT ARMAGEDDON

At least seven years later, probably more, things will be much more chaotic than immediately following the Rapture. God's judgments and Satan's rage will have pretty much wrecked the planet by the time all armies gather in the Middle East for man's last-gasp effort to defeat Christ. If Jesus doesn't directly intervene at that moment, He said, no one will survive.

The Tribulation saints who make it this far will have done so by the grace of the God who loves them, but they will indeed be a tough bunch. They will make pioneers of the American frontier look like Cub Scouts on a day trip to the zoo. These will be fit to enter and repopulate the Millennial Earth, which Jesus himself will totally refurbish and turn into a place much more beautiful than literature's Utopia.

Christ Can't Change

Jesus Christ, who is the second member of the Holy Trinity, can't change. "Jesus Christ is the same yesterday, today, and forever" (Hebrews 13:8). Neither can His message: "Repent and be saved." This is the business to which every believer of every era of human history has been assigned. Christians are to concern themselves with God's business of living for Christ, and telling the Good News (the Gospel of Christ).

BUSIEST OF THE BUSY

Christians in places where they are persecuted, tortured, and murdered—in places like China, Somalia, and the Sudan, just to name a few—know what it means to be about God's business. Their every waking moment is spent thinking about their Lord, and about reaching others of their countrymen for Him.

These are looking for Christ's coming for His Church, you can be sure. They are looking for Jesus' coming for them personally, as surely as those Tribulation saints will be counting the days until Christ's Second Advent. They will no doubt encourage each other daily with the words "Everybody *get* busy, Jesus is coming!"

END-TIME AILMENTS AND RAPTURE-READY RX

Bible Malnourishment Just as the lack of food will cause the human body to become physically weak, the lack of spiritual sustenance will result in a soul that is undeveloped.

Symptoms Someone suffering from this condition might not currently own a Bible, or does not know where his or her Bible is located. If the person does know where the Bible is, he or she has not opened it in several years. A quick test for Bible malnourishment is to ask someone to quote John 3:16.

Treatment Change reading diet to one that offers more meat from the Word of God. Relocate to a church that regularly preaches Bible-based messages. "And Jesus said to them, 'I am the bread of life. He who comes to Me shall never hunger, and he who believes in Me shall never thirst'" (John 6:35).

CHRIST'S
ON HIS WAY,
SO DON'T
STRAY!

CHAPTER 16

Your Final, Final, Final Warning

When Dr. Ben-Judah was finally able to quiet the crowd, he said, "Thank you for the warmth of your welcome, but I ask that in the future, when I am introduced, you do me the honor of merely silently thanking God for his love and mercy. That is what I will be talking about primarily, and whether you pray, raise your hands, or just point to the sky in acknowledgement of him, your adoration will be properly directed.

"In the fourteenth chapter of the Gospel of John, our Lord, Jesus the Messiah, makes a promise we can take to the bank of eternity. He says, 'Let not your heart be troubled; you believe in God, believe also in me. In my father's house are many mansions; if it were not so, I would have told you. I go to prepare a place for you. And if I go and prepare a place for you, I will come again and receive you unto myself; that where I am, there you may be also.'

"Notice the urgency. That was Jesus' guarantee that though he was leaving his disciples, one day he would return. The world had not seen the last of Jesus the Christ, and as many of you know, it still has not seen the last of him."

—The Remnant

WARNING WEARY

Americans, in particular, quickly grow weary of anything. We are a generation of instant gratification and constant entertainment. So it is with warnings. We quickly grow tired of those who preach warnings to us.

One of the greatest fears those charged with warning others about dangers have is the fear that people will become desensitized to the alerts they issue. Weather warnings come to mind. Sirens go off the first few times during spring in tornado-prone areas, and everyone's ears prick up. But when the storms turn out time after time to be only a little rain, thunder, and lightning, people begin to develop ho-hum attitudes, and instead of taking action to protect themselves, they go about business as usual when later sirens sound.

Since 9/11, much concern continues to be expressed about the terror alerts in America, as they involve homeland security. When attacks don't come, the collective national alert instinct is feared to diminish. Those charged with protecting American lives constantly seek ways to ensure the alert system is effective.

In One Ear and Out the Other

Warnings from prophecy preachers and teachers fall on deaf ears, for the most part, these days. But a time is coming when people will be eager to grasp at prophetic alerts from the Word of God. A group of people left behind in the novel *The Remnant* are alerted by Dr. Ben-Judah, a Jewish religious man who has become a believer in Christ during the Tribulation. He tells them again that Jesus is coming to make them part of His eternal kingdom.

The alert isn't just dismissed like so many warnings with which we are familiar today. In that day of Antichrist's regime, the believing group of people will grab onto all the talk of Jesus coming again they can get their ears on. It will be a time far worse than all of the pre-Rapture times of disaster combined.

Foretelling Terrible Times

How do we know that it will be a far worse time? By the words of Jesus, who repeated the words of the prophet Jeremiah in Jeremiah 30:7. Since it was Jesus who gave Jeremiah the words to write in the first place, we will use His prophecy, given on the Mount of Olives shortly before His crucifixion: "For then there will be great tribulation, such as has not been since the beginning of the world until this time, no, nor ever shall be" (Matthew 24:21).

Warnings to Left-Behind

The fictional characters left behind when the Rapture took place could have avoided going through that murderous time of Antichrist. Warnings of Christ's coming in the air above Earth for believers are prominent, especially in America. The LaHaye/Jenkins novels, for example, are there for millions to read and heed.

Hundreds of other books, most nonfiction explanations of prophecy and the Rapture, line the bookshelves of bookstores. True, not many preachers and teachers preach and teach that the Rapture could happen at any moment, but the warnings have been made.

Warning about Warnings

One of the biggest reasons for the lack of Rapture readiness has to be the fact that we are drowning in a sea of warning signs. Jesus warned about just such a time as this in which we live. He said: "So you also, when you see all these things, know that it is near—at the doors! Assuredly, I say to you, this generation will by no means pass away till all these things take place" (Matthew 24:33–34).

Final Warning Inc.

Prophetic authors have a natural tendency to aim for book titles that imply the direst scenarios. Dozens of books and sermons have "final warning" in their titles. It sounds catchy and clever, but when authors use the words "final warning," the implied message is that you should not expect any more warnings from the writer. For the sake

WALL-TO-WALL WARNINGS

Asahel Nettleton, a preacher who died in 1844, wrote a sermon entitled, "The Final Warning." More than 150 years later, we still have plenty of "final warning" books in print, and they are continuing to be published. Here are several book titles from just the past few years:

Final Warning
The Final Warning
The Final Warning: Your Survival Guide to the New Millennium
God's Trumpet Call: A Final Warning
Jesus' Final Warning
God's Final Warning to America
666: The Final Warning
The Last Day: The Final Warning
Final Warning: Daniel's Prophecies Decoded
A Final Warning to America

Upon talking to some of these authors, we found that most of them seemed to think it doesn't matter if the passage of time has thrown doubt upon their "final warning!" cries. They assert, for the most part, that their main goal was to make people aware of the approaching Endtime.

of continuity, if not honesty, any future books by the same writer should be given titles like "Final Warning 2," "Final Warning 3," or "More Final Warnings."

"Wolf! Wolf!"

In the story of the boy who cried wolf, the young lad was certainly active in warning the villagers, but we all know he eventually warned them a little too much. A final warning title may increase sales of books, but if the Lord Jesus doesn't return on the authors' cue, everyone who has read these books will be in danger of becoming immune to the end-time message. Perhaps that is one facet of the truth in the Apostle Peter's words: "Where is the promise of his coming? For since the fathers fell asleep, all things continue as they were from the beginning of creation" (2 Peter 3:4).

The mischievous shepherd boy who cried "Wolf!" repeatedly sent the townspeople running with his false alarms. When a real wolf finally did come prowling, no one responded to the boy's cry for help. There has been an increase of false cries of the prophetic kind in recent years. We're in the midst of a sharp increase in the number of false predictions concerning Jesus Christ's Second Coming. This trend indicates that Satan is attempting to suppress prophetic awareness. People have heard the sirens of overblown warnings so often that they less and less see the need to seek shelter from a storm they think will never come.

Picking on Predictors

It's always fascinating to take note of any new predictions, where some individual or group is claiming to know the exact time of Jesus Christ's return. Despite the fact that our Lord said, "Watch therefore, for you do not know what hour your Lord is coming" (Matthew 24:42), people are still trying to figure out the magic date.

DATE SETTING: THE DEVIL'S DELIGHT

One of the main reasons that the devil promotes date setting is that Bible prophecy already tells us what Satan's final plans are, and the devil knows he needs to discredit the Bible before he can fully set up his demonic kingdom.

Since every one of these predictions ends up being wrong, it's quite clear the devil is the one who originates them. False predictions certainly could not come from God's guidance: "When a prophet speaks in the name of the Lord, if the thing does not happen or come to pass, that is the thing which the Lord has not spoken . . ." (Deuteronomy 18:22).

Second-String Soothsayers

In the past, after someone forecasted Christ's return and was proven wrong, there traditionally followed a period of prophetic inactivity. People naturally become disillusioned after the uneventful date. However, today, as soon as one prognosticator fails, another quickly takes his place.

Back in the 1800s, a major Second Coming prediction appeared to occur about every thirty or forty years. In the 1970s and 80s, someone was claiming they knew when Jesus Christ was coming about every four years. Currently, we see a trend where predictions are being made several times a year.

End-Time Foretelling Fatigue

No other time in history had more signs pointing to Jesus' Second Coming than the present. Yet strangely, at the same time, end-time fatigue is also at very high levels. Even the way new dates are proclaimed shows the strain. Prognosticators at one time would openly set dates. Now because of the growing history of failed predictions, they just "suggest" dates.

Christians Castigated

Erroneous date setting has a profoundly negative affect on nonbelievers. The failings of Christians have always been a favorite excuse used by the lost to explain away their unsaved and unprepared condition. If you ask them, "Why don't you believe?" they'll point to crooked TV preachers. If you ask them, "Are you ready for Jesus' soon return?" they will tell you, "Oh, people have always been saying Jesus is coming soon."

FIND IT FAST

As it is with everyone who practices treachery, the devil has one huge problem. If people become aware of his true intentions, instead of his trickery working to deceive us, the devil's every act only works to warn us. Paul the apostle said that believers would not be in darkness (*Find It Fast*: 1 Thessalonians 5:4).

The Bible warns that as we draw closer to the end of the age, Satan will continue to trick people into crying, "Wolf!" As the cries grow louder, and folks in general become more desensitized toward the return of our Lord, we who are watchful for Jesus' return should be all the more watchful: "Therefore you also be

ready, for the Son of Man is coming at an hour you do not expect"
(Matthew 24:44).

JESUS IS COMING BACK—
BUT, PLEASE, NOT NOW!

When talking to unsaved people about the Rapture and world
events, statistics show that 90 percent of them agree with the validity of Bible prophecy. Most of them even admit that we are headed
toward the Tribulation hour. If you try to tell them we might be
getting near to the end, that's when you'll get strong opposition
from them. "Not in our lifetime" is the average reply.

When trying to reason with people about Christ's return, it's interesting to get their reaction by saying to them: "You agree Jesus is
coming back, and the likelihood of His return only increases each
year. Because there is nothing to prevent him from returning, why
not at least be open to the possibility to His coming in your time?"

A large portion of the population strongly refuses to consider
the prospect of prophecy being fulfilled in our generation. Sadly,
and tragically, in all honesty, these people probably have a good reason for not wanting to see the Endtime. The start of the Tribulation
would signal their doom.

Be a Winner!

In most wars where there are two main forces at odds with each
other, it's historically usual for fighters to realize they're on the losing side and defect to the side that's winning. This has been particularly true in tribal conflicts.

SEVEN-DAY WARNING

Have you ever wondered what would happen if the Lord super-naturally announced to the world that He was coming back in seven days? Of course, the proclamation would obviously have a profound impact on society:

- ⊕ Global stock markets would close.
- ⊕ Manufacturing would slow to a halt.
- ⊕ Stores would freely distribute their goods.
- ⊕ Livestock would be freed to roam the countryside.
- ⊕ It would be impossible to get an airline ticket to the Holy Land.
- ⊕ Prostitutes would become nuns overnight.
- ⊕ All media outlets would have continuous news coverage from Jerusalem.
- ⊕ A spirit of piety would sweep over the world.

FIND IT FAST

If you're not in Jesus' camp, you're on the losing team. For the time being, sinners still have the opportunity to abandon their loyalty to Satan and to realign with God. Once Jesus returns to Earth, it will become too late for someone to change his allegiance (*Find It Fast:* Revelation 6:15–17).

DATE SETTERS AND DOPES

During the Miller Movement of the 1840s, as people looked forward to Miller's predicted return of Christ, a number of people did things they later regretted. When the date failed to produce the Lord Jesus or doomsday, most folks went right back to their previous sinful lifestyles. The fact that people would make phony commitments immediately ahead of a known Rapture date is the most likely reason the Bible says we shouldn't expect a prior warning.

THE WINDOW OF OPPORTUNITY

People will be able to calculate exactly when Jesus is coming back to Earth during the Tribulation. From the time the Antichrist declares himself to be God, saints will know that the Second Coming will take place in forty-two months (*Find It Fast*: Revelation 13:5).

FIND IT FAST

An obvious question some folks might ask: Why is the timing of the Rapture a big secret, while the timing of the Second Coming is an obvious giveaway? The answer is simple: For the most part, it currently doesn't cost the average person much to live for Christ. The unknown time of His any-moment return should motivate and give incentive to Christians who are not being physically persecuted to want to be ready for His sudden appearing.

Once the Tribulation starts, however, all believers will be in a whole new ball game. Most will have to suffer martyrdom to hold onto their Christian faith. Those believers will desperately long for His return. They will definitely be ready! Contemplating how bad it is going to be for those left behind, any benefit people of the Tribulation might derive from knowing when the Tribulation will end is certainly nothing to envy.

SECOND CHANCE?

A few Bible scholars go to the extreme by promoting the idea that it will be impossible for people to find salvation after the Rapture. Their general attitude seems to be if you're foolish enough to miss the Rapture, you should be out of luck.

Once a person finds himself left behind, his flesh might be in a dreadful state of affairs, but as long as he draws breath and he doesn't take Antichrist's mark, his soul still has a chance for redemption. We believe God's Word teaches there will be a second chance for people during the Tribulation.

WARNING ABOUT WAITING

FIND IT FAST

On the other hand, it is very difficult to try to understand where people get the idea that the Tribulation is going to allow believers to blissfully wait for Jesus to come and rescue them. Since the Tribulation is going to be a time of immense persecution, few people realize we are living in a window of opportunity that will soon close. Most of the saints who will find salvation after the Rapture will not physically live to see Jesus' glorious return (*Find It Fast:* Revelation 13:7, 10).

Because man has no control over his destiny, however, it's foolhardy for him to somehow think that he will have other opportunities to turn his life over to Jesus. You have no guarantee you will be here tomorrow. Therefore, it should be obvious that you need to be ready today.

NO SUCH THING AS A FINAL WARNING

We could say, as other people do, that this could be the last time you encounter the message that Jesus is the one and only way to salvation. But that would only be speculation on our part. You might be presented with the salvation message a hundred times after you read this book.

Survival and Spiritual Status Unsure

The aging process tells us a twenty-year-old man has a greater chance of being around a year from now than a ninety-year-old man. However, unless the older gentleman is in declining health, it's unlikely he's going to have a deeper focus on his spiritual state than the man who's still a youngster. If someone is ninety years old, he expects to live to see ninety-one. If he makes it to ninety-nine, he generally believes he'll make it to one hundred.

Death is always a surprise. Because there is no certainty you're going to be here tomorrow, you need to accept Jesus as your eternal Savior today. To do this you first must ask Jesus to forgive you of your sins: "Repent therefore and be converted, that your sins may be blotted out, so that times of refreshing may come from the presence of the Lord" (Acts 3:19); "Nor is there salvation in any other, for there is no other name under heaven given among men by which we must be saved" (Acts 4:12).

After you commit yourself in words to Jesus, you then begin to follow Him with your actions. This includes reading His Word, the

Bible, and praying. God, the Holy Spirit, will lead you into a life filled with joy, peace, and service for Him.

FINAL WARNINGS FACTS

There once was a big-time evangelist who visited a large city in central Africa. During one crusade service, over ten thousand people raised hands to show that they had accepted Jesus into their lives. Several months later, a Christian organization did a follow-up study. They found that less than 1 percent of those people were still practicing their faith. The other 99 percent had heard the warning message, but they must have assumed that in the future they would yet be offered a final, final warning or possibly a final, final, final warning. In actuality, the last warning you received is the only one you can count on. There are no guarantees beyond that.

To be Rapture ready is to be alert to the any-moment call of Christ. Whether the Lord calls in the great disappearance, or whether He calls in death, you must truly be born again to be prepared. "Behold, now is the accepted time; behold, now is the day of salvation" (2 Corinthians 6:2).

THE BEGINNING IS NEAR!

Conclusion

Then the seventh angel sounded: And there were loud voices in heaven, saying, "The kingdoms of this world have become the kingdoms of our Lord and of His Christ, and He shall reign forever and ever!"

—Revelation 11:15

THE BEGINNING IS NEAR!

There is great news in all of this talk of Tribulation, Antichrist, and Armageddon. What we are seeing on the horizon of history at present is not the beginning of the end. It is just the end of the beginning.

Being Rapture ready means much, much more than merely escaping the great destruction and devastation prophetically scheduled for those last seven years. Being Rapture ready means getting a jump on attaining heavenly citizenship. Those who are raptured will instantaneously begin living eternal, supernatural lives in heavenly homes prepared by Christ, himself, as promised in John 14:1–6.

BETTER LATE THAN NEVER

Tribulation saints who live through the carnage will join the raptured believers following the return of Christ. They will be ushered into national homelands of a beautifully restored Planet Earth.

However, these will be earthly beings, while the raptured and all others who lived and died as believers will be heavenly beings. Jesus will be the King, and His rule will be absolute. His earthly reign of one thousand years will not be a cruel dictatorship. It will be a loving, magnificent reign of perfect righteousness.

RAPTURED TO RULE

Those who are raptured (both the resurrected dead and living believers of the Church Age) will be assigned as rulers within Christ's kingdom administration throughout the Earth and all of God's universes, the Bible says: "Blessed and holy is he who has part in the first resurrection. Over such the second death has no power, but they shall be priests of God and of Christ, and shall reign with him a thousand years" (Revelation 20:6).

NO LOCKED DOORS

The need for locking doors during Christ's millennial reign will be eliminated. Men and women can still commit sin, and crime will still be possible. Those things that made the old Earth get worse and worse until it had to be judged by God, however, will be dealt with instantly, when they are committed. The guilty will be removed, unless they truly repent. And Christ, the all-knowing judge of all things, will know the truly innocent and the truly repentant from the guilty and unrepentant.

WHY IS THERE STILL SIN?

If Christ will make the Earth perfect again, why do people still sin? is a question that many ask. It's a good one. The answer, in brief, is that although Christ is present in person, and nobody can get away with any crime or sin, men and women can still sin. They still have the "sin nature" they inherited from their father, the first man, Adam.

As a matter of fact, millions of people born during this time will harbor sinful thoughts. They will, for the most part, exercise the discipline necessary to keep from acting on their desires. They will do so out of knowledge they will be found out and punished if they carry out their sinful thoughts. Remember, these people who repopulate the planet following Christ's return at the time of Armageddon are flesh and blood. They have to be in order to have children.

PEOPLE OF PERFECTION

Jesus' words tell this truth about those who are no longer flesh-and-blood beings, but are now heavenly citizens: "For in the resurrection they neither marry nor are given in marriage, but are like angels of God in heaven" (Matthew 22:30). This doesn't mean people in Heaven are sexless; it simply means that repopulating their realm is unnecessary.

The flesh-and-blood folks who go into the thousand-year era of Christ's reign on Earth can never lose their salvation. Their souls are secured for eternity. But the sin-polluted bloodline still flows within their flesh. Therefore, their offspring—and there will most likely be billions—will still have a "sin nature," which man inherited from Adam. Only Christ can remove this, through belief in His death, burial, and resurrection.

These people born during the Millennium must make the same choice their fathers and mothers made during the Tribulation. They must believe in Jesus Christ. When they do, they will be children of God forever.

REBELLION RISES AGAIN

Prophecy says that millions will rebel, proving that even though Jesus himself sits upon the throne of a Garden of Eden–like Earth, man is still fallen, because of Adam's original sin.

Satan will have been chained in the abyss, a region somewhere within the Earth. His confinement will end somewhere near the end of Christ's thousand-year reign.

REVELATION 20:1–3, 7–10

Satan will seethe with rage in his chains at the bottom of the bottomless pit. Neither he nor his demonic forces will be granted the privilege of influencing humanity in any way during his period of confinement. Then the devil will be released, and he immediately will go forth and deceive all who are not believers. He will gather a force of millions to try to take the throne from Christ and reestablish himself as Earth's ruler.

Rebellion Rebuffed

God will put down the rebellion even quicker than He defeated Antichrist's forces. Satan and his rebel angels will all be cast into hell, a place burning with fire and brimstone. He will be the third person placed there. The first two are Antichrist and the False Prophet.

WHY IN THE WORLD?

It's proper to ask: Why would God release this monster?

The answer one theologian gave was "If you tell me why God let him loose in the first place, I'll tell you why He let him loose in the second place."

PROOF IN THE REBELLION

Truth is, nobody really knows why Satan will be released. But most who study these matters believe it will be to prove once and for all humanity's lost condition, to show that, indeed, man still has a fallen nature because of Adam's disobedience in the Garden of Eden.

Despite Jesus himself ruling on Earth, and the Earth being in perfect condition, with prosperity and plenty everywhere, man will still choose to follow Satan when he comes forth to lead yet another rebellion.

WHITE THRONE JUDGMENT

All the rebels of all the ages since the time of Adam and Eve will be called forth. They will, individually, stand before God, who will sit upon what is termed a "great white throne." The prophecy says:

"Then I saw a great white throne and Him who sat on it, from whose face the earth and the heavens fled away. And there was found no place for them. And I saw the dead, small and great, standing before God, and books were opened. And another book was opened, which is the Book of Life. And the dead were judged according to their works, by the things which were written in the books. The sea gave up the dead who were in it, and Death and Hades delivered up the dead who were in them. And they were judged, each one according to his works. Then Death and Hades were cast into the lake of fire. This is the second death. And anyone not found written in the Book of Life was cast into the lake of fire" (Revelation 20:11–15).

There are no believers at this judgment, except as observers of

God's perfect justice and righteousness. God will look in the "Lamb's Book of Life." Those standing before God will be told their names are not in the book. They will be judged lost for eternity. All who appear before God in this judgment will be cast alive, in eternal, indestructible bodies, into the Lake of Fire, a place that was not prepared for humans, but for Lucifer and the angels who rebelled with him.

YOU MAKE THE CHOICE

These lost humans chose to follow Satan. They did so by rejecting Jesus and His offer of redemption through His sacrifice on the cross. Now the lost must face eternity apart from God. Every memory of them will be erased.

Beginning Really Begins

With Satan sentenced to eternity in hell, along with the False Prophet and Antichrist, the Earth will be completely reshaped and remade for an eternity in oneness with God. That is, all will again be in perfect unity with God and all believers of all ages.

About this, the Bible says: "Now I saw a new heaven and a new earth, for the first heaven and the first earth had passed away . . . And God will wipe away every tear from their eyes; there shall be no more death, nor sorrow, nor crying. There shall be no more pain, for the former things have passed away" (Revelation 21:1–4).

RAPTURE READY—NOT ROBOTS

God didn't create robots when He created man. Every person who has ever lived has had free will to choose how he or she will live, the disposition of his or her soul upon facing death, and how he or she will spend eternity.

Those who are Rapture ready have chosen to live in expectation of Christ's any-moment coming for them. Theirs are decisions that will have glorious eternal consequences. Jesus, who gave John the prophet and apostle the Revelation, told the old man to write: "He who is unjust, let him be unjust still; he who is filthy, let him be filthy still; he who is righteous, let him be righteous still; he who is holy, let him be holy still.

"And behold, I am coming quickly; and My reward is with Me, to give to every one according to his work. I am the Alpha and the Omega, the Beginning and the End, the First and the Last.

"Blessed are those who do His commandments, that they may have right to the tree of life, and may enter in through the gates into the city" (Revelation 22:11–14).

Being Rapture ready is not an act of fear that looks for an angry God who hates mankind. Being Rapture ready means being prepared for an instantaneous new beginning which is promised by God, who loves mankind so much He gave His Son to die so we can live forever in His presence.

ABOUT THE AUTHORS

Todd Strandberg started the Rapture Ready organization in 1987, which has been featured by the *New York Times, Rolling Stone, Time* magazine, *Wired,* and *Inside Edition,* among other prominent publications and media outlets. He is a member of the PreTrib Study Center, a think tank of writers, broadcasters, and scholars. He lives in Nebraska.

William "Terry" James is the author of many books on Bible prophecy and is frequently interviewed on TV, radio, and in print media about prophetic matters. He is a lecturer on eschatology (the study of the Endtime). He lives in Arkansas.